garden feast
Melissa King

photography by Virginia Cummins

APPLE

CONTENTS

Introduction

It's been a dream of mine to write this book and bring together the two things I'm most passionate about—gardens and food. For most of us, preparing a meal begins with flipping through recipe books then heading off to the shops for the necessary ingredients. When you grow your own fruit, vegetables and herbs at home, this situation is reversed. Instead you're faced with a selection of fresh, seasonal ingredients, picked straight from the garden, and the wonderful dilemma of what to cook with them. The garden becomes your inspiration.

I get so much pleasure from growing and eating my own food and I want to inspire a new generation of gardeners to do the same. I know not everyone has the luxury of space or the time to create a totally self-sufficient garden—I certainly don't—but I encourage everyone to have a go at growing at least a few edible plants at home. I have been in situations where all I was able to grow was a small selection of herbs, leafy greens and cherry tomatoes in pots, but the reward was months of fresh, spectacular tasting salads.

There has never been an easier time to begin experimenting with a kitchen garden. Nurseries and garden centres are filled with a diverse assortment of vegetable seedlings, herbs, vines and fruit trees, and seeds can be purchased from virtually every supermarket and grocer, and even via mail order. These provide plenty of options for both the novice and experienced gardener alike, but for me there is nothing more inspiring than turning back time and rediscovering traditional varieties which have been preserved and valued by generations of gardeners.

I have focused much of this book on these 'antique', or 'heirloom', varieties. They are sometimes a little harder to source, but the sheer thrill of growing something different and introducing your tastebuds to an amazing new palette of flavours and textures is well worth the effort. Knowing that you are contributing to the conservation of precious heirloom varieties can be yet another rewarding aspect of growing fruit and vegetables in your own backyard.

Travel to the Digger's Club gardens at Heronswood on the Mornington Peninsula in Victoria, Australia and you'll discover a wonderful example of an edible garden showcasing the diversity and beauty of heirloom produce.

I will never forget visiting the garden for the first time. I had never seen, let alone tasted, anything other than red, and occasionally yellow, tomatoes. At Heronswood, the gardens were not only filled with a diverse assortment of spectacular-looking tomatoes, but with heirloom vegetables of all manner of unusual shape, size and colour. It was the start of a beautiful affair. It inspired me to track down old nursery catalogues and to try to unearth varieties that once existed. I soon found myself experimenting with different fruits and vegetables that I had never grown or cooked with before.

Clive and Penny Blazey, founders of Digger's Club and the owners of Heronswood, have long been staunch advocates for heirloom produce, dedicating almost three decades to sourcing, preserving and introducing gardeners to some of the best old-fashioned varieties, based on their extensive experience of growing and cooking with them. I was delighted when the team of horticulturalists and chefs at Heronswood agreed to work closely with me on this book to help select some of the best varieties for the home gardener, and to develop some sumptuous recipes that make the most of their dazzling colours and flavours—a true feast for the eyes and the tastebuds!

Flavour is what inspires many people to grow their own fruit and vegetables. I don't know how many times I have been seduced by the rich colours and perfect appearance of supermarket produce, only to be bitterly disappointed by the flavour—or lack thereof. In my childhood garden we had an old apricot tree. Each year, without doing much at all, we enjoyed a bountiful crop of delectably sweet fruit. Nothing

Flavour is what
inspires many
people to grow
their own fruit
and vegetables

store-bought can ever match that taste for me. Tomatoes are another classic example. The ones you buy from the shops are so often rubbery and tasteless, and can never compare to biting into a delicious vine-ripened tomato straight from the garden.

Abundant quantity, reliable appearance and constant availability are important commercial drivers, resulting in the ever-increasing use of genetically modified or hybrid crops, the excessive application of synthetic fertilisers and pesticides, a reliance on artificial growing and ripening conditions, the prolonged storage of produce and the need to transport this produce often thousands of kilometres to reach its point of sale. With consistency, durability and supply being the overriding imperatives, we're destined to experience the 'looks great but tastes lousy' scenario for a long time yet.

To be fair, the diversity of varieties available and the flavour of store-bought produce is improving, but the circumstances described above are still cause for alarm. Most of us are so divorced from what we eat that we are quite unaware of the journey our favourite fruit and vegetables have been on to reach our plate. I don't know about you, but I would much prefer a tasty crop with a few imperfections than chemically drenched, blemish-free fruit and vegetables that lack flavour. When you grow tasty, seasonally relevant, organic produce at home you'll have an intimate knowledge of each plant's journey from seed to table, and you'll get to enjoy the rewards of lovingly nurtured crops where 'freshness' literally means 'picked only moments before'.

Establishing a kitchen garden is an investment in your health. Science has long touted what we were told as kids—eat lots of fruit and vegetables and you'll grow up healthy and strong. Fruit and vegetables are packed full of vitamins, minerals and trace elements that are essential for the preservation of life and the maintenance of good health. They control chemical reactions in our bodies and regulate many body systems. They support vital body functions, including the conversion of food to energy, the maintenance and repair of body tissues, building strong bones and teeth, transmitting nerve signals, maintaining a normal heartbeat, and the production of blood cells, enzymes, hormones and essential fatty acids.

In more recent times, science has shifted its attention to nature's very own defensive chemicals, 'antioxidants', which have been shown to provide significant protection against many common diseases. Oxidation is a damaging process caused by a group of chemicals known as free radicals, which are released when our bodies burn the oxygen we breathe, or through exposure to outside influences such as smoking, environmental pollution, ultraviolet radiation, and chemical contact with our skin. These free radicals circulate throughout our bodies, attaching themselves to healthy cells and causing damage that can lead to premature ageing and disease.

Enter the 'antioxidant police', natural chemicals that we get from the food we eat, which patrol our bodies to neutralise the destructive potential of the free radicals. Vitamins A, C and E are some of the better known antioxidants, but there are also thousands of phytochemicals (from the Greek *phyton* for 'plant') that are believed to have powerful antioxidant and other disease-fighting properties. The most powerfully protective group of natural food chemicals comes from the hundreds of different pigments that have been identified in plants. All fruits and vegetables will offer benefit, but it is those that are deeply coloured—dark green, deep red, purple, yellow and bright orange—that have the highest levels. An edible garden not only supplies superior tasting produce, but is also your very own natural pharmacy.

The kitchen garden

There is nothing simpler, nor more beautiful, than a kitchen garden.
Saint Ignatius, 1491–1556

Although spoken almost 500 years ago, these astute words are still relevant for the contemporary kitchen garden. There are so many opportunities for introducing edible plants to the modern garden. Fruit and vegetables can be grown among annuals and perennials in a herbaceous border or in dedicated beds or plots. There are trees that provide shade and shelter with the bonus of delectable fruit. There are fruiting vines that will cover fences or climb pergolas, and there are compact edible plants that are perfect for tubs and containers.

Some edible plants have a reputation among gardeners for being aesthetically unappealing, but fruit, vegetables and herbs mingled with flowers can be a feast for the eyes as well as for the tastebuds. Heirloom varieties in particular bring a diversity of colours, textures and forms to the garden, which rival the beauty and ornamental value of any flower.

There is also a perception that kitchen gardens can be overly complicated. There are optimal conditions and gardening techniques that apply to all plants, and some gardeners may get bogged down with soil testing, watering systems, fertilising regimes and other more technical pursuits. Yet I have known plenty of people who achieve outstanding results simply by sowing the seeds and adding water.

As with any gardening, being well prepared, following some basic techniques and putting in a bit of hard work will increase your chances of success. Fruit and vegetables generally need a sunny position in the garden that gets at least six hours of sunlight per day. Thorough soil preparation is well worth the effort. Most edible plants enjoy a rich, well-drained loamy soil, with plenty of organic material worked in to replenish nutrients and create the ideal medium for plant growth.

Most fruits and vegetables require a fair amount of water, particularly leafy vegetables and fast-growing cut-and-come-again varieties. A deep watering to the base of plants two or three times a week is far superior to a superficial spray over the plot every day. Drip-based watering systems or perforated hosing that can be curled between plants on the ground are viable options, but hand-watering will do the job. Plants in containers may require more frequent watering as the soil tends to dry out more quickly. Using a good-quality potting mix and water-retaining crystals are highly recommended.

A decent application of mulch around your plants will help conserve moisture and suppress weeds. For a productive garden, I would recommend organic mulch like pea straw or lucerne, which will nourish and enrich the soil as it breaks down. Apply

mulch in a layer about 10 centimetres thick, but not too close to the stems or trunks as this may cause rotting.

One of the best things about growing your own food is regaining control over what you're eating. As long as you're prepared to put up with a few blemishes, there is no reason why you can't grow your fruit and vegetables without the use of synthetic fertilisers, herbicides and pesticides. An organic approach is perfectly viable for the home gardener, but it is ultimately a decision for each individual. I have provided some general organic growing information throughout this book, and there are lots of books dedicated to this subject for those wishing to learn more.

Nature's bounty is so impressive. You can get so much from just a single handful of seed. A packet of seed will grow enough to feed you and your family, with plenty left over to give away or store. And one of the great joys of gardening is being able to collect seed to grow again the following year—a pleasure lost with modern hybrids which do not produce the same plants from their seed.

Gardening crosses barriers of age in a way that few other pastimes can. I can't think of any other pursuit that my niece enjoys as much as my grandmother does. I have always believed that gardening is a part of our education and that children, particularly, need to make the vital connection between growing and eating food so they know that apples do not grow in supermarkets. Growing fruits and vegetables is a great way to introduce children to the joys of gardening and to encourage their appreciation of fresh, healthy food.

About 'Garden Feast'

Research suggests that less than 5 per cent of all fruits and vegetables consumed come from the home garden. My aim with this book is to inspire and motivate people to have a go at growing at least a few edible plants at home. I can't hope to write about all the fruits and vegetables that I consider worthy or have grown over the years, but this book isn't intended to be an encyclopaedia of varieties—other books do a much better job of that. Instead, I have chosen to write about a selection of some of my favourite old-fashioned varieties, which are proven performers in the home garden. Each chapter focuses on a different selection, providing practical information and advice on how to achieve the best results in your garden.

This book is not a technical manual, but rather provides some guidelines that will hopefully kick-start your enthusiasm for the wonders of kitchen gardening. Trying some of the options in this book is only the beginning of the journey. The excitement and confidence that comes with your first harvest may be the impetus for trying some of the thousands of other varieties that are now available to us all. You may not succeed with everything, but I'm a firm believer that experimentation and trial and error are an inevitable part of our gardening experience, and an essential element of the learning process.

Gardening and cooking are such natural companions. Old-fashioned flavour has never been quite as prominent in the modern cooking arena as it is right now. This is reinforced by the number of top restaurateurs and chefs who are turning to heirloom varieties to bring a little pizazz and lots of extra flavour to their dishes. Toss a selection of black, red, yellow and green tomatoes together in a bowl and you'll impress even the most discerning guests. Then think purple carrots, white and burgundy striped aubergines, golden beets and spotted lettuce; the potential for culinary creativity is limited only by your imagination.

I certainly don't profess to be a gourmet chef, but I do enjoy cooking and eating great food—and the best starting point is fresh, garden-grown ingredients. To highlight the true value of a kitchen garden, the team from the Heronswood Café has developed some mouth-watering recipes that are included at the end of each chapter, showcasing the flavours, textures and colours of heirloom produce. Most of these tantalising recipes have been designed for maximum flavour with minimum degree of difficulty, suitable for even the absolute novice in the kitchen. A few culinary challenges have also been included for those more confident and adventurous cooks.

Heirloom varieties

A few years ago, a friend gave me some seeds of the Chioggia beetroot, named after a small town overlooking the Venetian lagoon. In the catalogue it was described as an heirloom variety with pink rings and white flesh, just like an onion. I'd never seen anything like it. It grew easily, thriving in a sunny spot with rich soil, and boasted a wonderfully sweet flavour. It turns out that beetroot comes in all colours, shapes and sizes. So do beans, peas, carrots, tomatoes, eggplant, lettuce, potatoes and sweet corn. Heirloom vegetables are more than just a talking point, they are garden-worthy varieties that have stood the test of time—and they're delicious too.

What is an heirloom variety?

Generally, the label 'heirloom' is applied to vegetables introduced before World War Two. The cut-off date is somewhat arbitrary, but it does predate the development of most popular hybrids. Many heirloom vegetables can be traced back 100 to 150 years, and some even further.

Early seed catalogues were filled with varieties that had been valued and preserved for generations, many of which disappeared from the seed trade as commercial companies dumped them for modern varieties. With a desire to recapture the tastes and memories of the past there has been a major resurgence in the popularity of these old-fashioned varieties among many home gardeners.

Beauty and flavour

Why be content with orange carrots when you can have purple, white and yellow ones too? Heirloom varieties bring flamboyancy to both the garden and the table, with their extraordinary shapes, colours, textures and forms providing magical displays and far superior taste. It's no wonder they have become the produce of choice for many top restaurants.

The slow-food movement has also been instrumental in the revival of many heirloom varieties. Beginning in Italy in response to the proliferation of fast-food outlets, there are now slow-food groups throughout the world, with devotees numbering well over 100,000. The slow-food philosophy is all about the use of fresh, locally grown seasonal produce, which is slowly and lovingly prepared in an array of dishes that truly exploit the wonderful flavours on offer, then usually enjoyed in communion with others.

Heirloom varieties sit at the very heart of this movement. Slow-food gatherings are often a celebration of varieties that have their very origins in that particular region. Carefully selected for their superior taste and performance, these varieties have been saved and passed on by generations of gardeners. This diligent commitment to their preservation provides an implicit seal of approval— a promise of something unique.

Garden treasures

Heirloom vegetables are genuine garden performers. Garden trials have shown that they are reliable, productive, tasty, easy to grow, and equal to their modern counterparts when it comes to pest and disease resistance. Unlike some of the modern varieties which tend to give you a glut of mature produce all at once, heirloom varieties will often provide you with fresh produce over many weeks or months.

They also offer important glimpses into our cultural heritage and provide a reservoir of genetic traits for future use. Desirable traits such as taste, colour, productivity, and disease and pest resistance can be bred into modern varieties from these old staples, rather than by using gene technologies that threaten the organic status of nearby crops.

Using genetic diversity, rather than technology, to improve crops also protects against unexpected problems. The Irish potato famine (1845–48), which saw a million people die of starvation and disease, was caused by potato blight (*phytophthora infestans*) that had been imported from Mexico. Almost the entire Irish potato crop consisted of only two varieties of potato, both of which were unable to resist the blight. Records show that fifty years before, Irish farmers had been growing over a dozen varieties of potato, some of which may have been resistant to the disease.

Heirloom vegetables are open-pollinated varieties, which means they will grow 'true to type' from their seed. Their seed can be collected and saved year after year, unlike hybrids which won't produce the same plants from their seed. And like other precious heirlooms, their histories and stories can be passed down through generations.

Seed saving

The traditional practice of gathering and saving seed for the following season's crop has resulted in well-adapted varieties with good cropping ability and, above all, flavour.

Most heirloom varieties allow you to collect seed year after year. It isn't hard to do. Always select the strongest, healthiest and tastiest plants to save seed from. Let some of the best looking leafy and root vegetables run to seed, and for fruiting vegetables, such as tomatoes and pumpkins, leave the best fruits on the vine until they are fully ripe.

Allow the seeds of leafy, root and bean-type vegetables to fully mature and dry before you harvest them. Cut the seed heads after a few dry days and hang them upside down against the inside of a bucket so the seeds can be collected easily. They can also be brought inside for the final stages of drying if there is a risk of rain. Hang them upside down with a paper bag over the seed head or pod until they are dry and ready for collection. It's a good idea to add a sachet of silica (available from chemists) to the bag to prevent mould.

For tomatoes and capsicums, pick the fruit when a little over-ripe. For melons and pumpkins, pick at the same time as you would for eating, but allow them to mature for another three weeks or so. For all of these vegetables, scoop the seeds out of the flesh, wash in a fine strainer under warm running water and leave to dry on a paper towel for several days.

Vegetable seeds can remain viable for about three to five years if they're stored correctly in an airtight glass jar and placed in a cool, dry position. If you plan to sow them in the near future, you can store them in paper bags or envelopes in a cool, dry, dark position or in the fridge.

PRESERVING OUR HERITAGE

At the turn of the last century, people grew their own vegetables from seeds collected from the best of the previous season's crop. The origins of this seed often dated back generations, collected and passed on for their superior productivity, taste, length of cropping and storage capacity.

With the advent of supermarkets and refrigeration many people stopped growing their own produce and turned to the convenience offered by the marketplace. Retailers increasingly abandoned heirloom varieties in favour of hybrids, which promised consistent supply, longer shelf life and uniform size and appearance. Driven by the bottom line, flavour barely came into consideration. With the demand no longer there and the numbers of home producers in decline, many old varieties simply disappeared.

However, thanks to seed-saving networks throughout the world, many of the heirloom varieties live on. It's now up to a new generation of gardeners to support their ongoing survival and keep their heritage alive!

Tomatoes

Tasty tomatoes have deservedly become one of the mainstays of home vegetable gardens. They are easy to grow, productive and versatile in the kitchen—that's what makes them such an irresistible choice! Once you have sampled delicious vine-ripened tomatoes, there's definitely no going back to store-bought options.

My sister-in-law's parents come from Italy, and some years ago she introduced me to some fantastic heirloom tomatoes with a basketful of home-grown varieties, all exotically named and wonderfully tasty. These tomato varieties had been grown by her mother and grandmother, passed down from one generation to the next.

My father does the same thing. When I was young I remember sneaking off into our vegetable garden to snack on our ripe crop of tiny red tomatoes. Dad still grows the same unnamed variety that my grandparents grew, and he collects the seed every year, not just for the sentimental value but because it's a delicious, sweet, genuinely good performer. These are just two examples of a wise gardening practice that's been going on for centuries.

The tomato (*Lycopersicon esculentum*) originates from South America and is a member of the Solanaceae family. In the wild, this is a variable species with tiny bite-sized fruit. Over the generations its popularity and productivity inspired growers to develop a diverse range of varieties. Wherever it was introduced, locally bred types with different tolerances, shapes, sizes, colours and flavours emerged, resulting in an impressive roll call of tomato types.

Most tomatoes you would commonly see in the shops have been developed to have tougher skins, uniform shape, colour and ripening, as well as an improved storage and shelf life, often at the expense of flavour. Over the years this focus on commercial priorities has seen the disappearance of many of the heirloom varieties. Many home gardeners have returned to these varieties, not only to capture the traditional taste, but also for benefits such as longer cropping times or early- or late-ripening crops. So why confine yourself to boring, round, red tomatoes when you can choose from Italian, Russian, French or South American tomatoes in greens, yellows, pinks, reds and even blacks, and a diversity of shapes and sizes?

Heirloom tomatoes are garden-worthy varieties that have stood the test of time. They have been selected and saved by generations of gardeners, often because of their outstanding taste, good cropping power or unique flavours, textures or colours.

Health and nutrition

Tomatoes contain large amounts of vitamin C and are a good source of vitamin A, potassium, iron and vitamin E. It is the phytochemical, lycopene, however, which is perhaps grabbing the most attention when it comes to the health-promoting claims of the tomato. In regard to phytochemical research, few things have been more extensively studied than lycopene. A number of international studies exploring the effects of lycopene on humans have revealed its extraordinary antioxidant ability, with claims that it may have 'twice the punch' as other well-known antioxidants, such as beta-carotene. Studies have linked lycopene to the prevention or inhibition of a growing list of cancers and diseases, including prostate, colon, breast, endometrial, lung and pancreatic cancers, cardiovascular disease and strokes. It is believed that such benefits are further enhanced by the synergy between lycopene and other phytochemicals naturally present in tomatoes, meaning that eating a fresh tomato is probably a much better option than taking lycopene as a supplement.

THE PROOF IS IN THE TASTING...

Tomatoes are members of the deadly nightshade family. When brought to Europe in the 16th century, tomatoes were considered to be poisonous and were only used ornamentally. In the United States tomatoes weren't eaten until the early 1800s. On 26 September 1820, in his hometown of Salem, an eccentric American, Colonel Robert Gibbon Johnson, publicly consumed an entire basket of tomatoes that he had brought back from a trip overseas. The shocked crowd of spectators anxiously waited to see if he would keel over. Of course, he didn't, and tomatoes have gone on to become the most consumed vegetable in the United States.

Growing

The best thing about growing heirloom tomatoes is that you can experiment with many types that aren't available in supermarkets.

Heirloom tomatoes are warm-season, frost-susceptible plants. In cooler areas, plant out seedlings after the risk of frost has passed—March to May, depending on your climate. In cold climates, you can

start tomatoes under glass, in pots or seed trays, by growing seeds six to eight weeks before the last frost.

Tomatoes require a well-drained, open and sunny spot in the garden—at least six hours of sun per day is ideal. Generally, fruit will not develop properly if night temperatures fall below 12 degrees Celsius or day temperatures go above 30 degrees—but don't be obsessed about bringing out the thermometer because few gardeners ever fail with tomatoes.

Before planting, dig an area around 60 centimetres deep, incorporating plenty of compost into the soil. Avoid the temptation to add excessive amounts of animal manure as high nitrogen levels will encourage leaf growth rather than flower and fruit formation. Tomatoes like a soil pH between 6 and 8. If your soil is too acidic, sprinkle a handful or two of lime or dolomite per square metre onto the soil before planting. Lime will also help prevent blossom-end rot developing.

Be generous with your spacing. Tomatoes need room for their roots to spread, providing stability for the plant and improved access to water and nutrients in stressful periods. More compact varieties will obviously need less space—so check labels or growing instructions for specific recommendations. Tomato plants can root along the stem, so seedlings can be planted deeper than normal to encourage a larger root ball and a stable start.

Apply an organic mulch to suppress weeds and help conserve moisture. Tomatoes require regular and deep watering. Apply water to the base of the plant rather than the leaves, and avoid over-watering as this increases the incidence of fungal problems.

Most heirloom tomatoes have a vine-like growth habit to 1.5–2.5 metres tall and need some support to grow on. Add the support at planting time to prevent disturbing the roots of older plants. As the plants grow, tie them to the stake or climbing frame using a soft cloth or twine in a figure-eight.

There is passionate debate both for and against the pruning of tomato plants. Pruning reduces yields but can encourage early ripening, especially in cooler climates. In humid conditions, such as glasshouses, it can also be a good technique for increasing air circulation around plants. Some gardeners choose not to prune to reduce disease entry points and promote higher yields. For the record, I rarely bother pruning and am more than happy with the results I get.

Tomatoes are the one crop that I always rotate to reduce disease build-up. If at all possible, try not to plant tomatoes in the same bed for at least two years.

Harvest

Heirloom tomatoes tend to crop over a longer period than hybrids, providing a steady supply of ripe, tasty fruit for up to four months. Ideally, pick your fruit when the skin has changed to its mature colour to maximise sweetness. As delicious as vine-ripened tomatoes are, many gardeners face serious competition from birds. You could apply bird netting over your plants, pick the fruit early to continue its ripening off the vine or grow tasty varieties like Green Zebra, which is unattractive to birds. More often than not you'll get a crop substantial enough to feed you, your family *and* the birds!

PRESERVING THE PAST BY SAVING SEEDS FOR THE FUTURE

Such is the popularity of the tomato that at the turn of the 20th century more than 4000 varieties had been recorded. Sadly, many of these have now been lost. Seed savers' groups and networks play an invaluable role in conserving our fruit and vegetable heritage, but the best way to ensure we don't lose traditional varieties is to plant them in our gardens.

Theoretically, you only have to buy heirloom tomato seeds once, as long as you save the seed. Save seeds from the strongest, healthiest, most flavoursome crops and share them with your friends and family. The more friends and family members you give them to, the greater the chance of a variety's survival.

Scrape the seeds from three or four ripe tomatoes into a small container and add a small amount of water—enough to wet them. Set it aside for about four days to allow the mixture to ferment (until it has developed skin or mould on top). Wash the mixture in a fine sieve under running water, and spread the seed out in a fine layer on paper towel or newspaper to dry. Seeds can be stored for up to five years if kept in a cool, dry environment in a sealed jar. Let them mature for three months before sowing.

Heirloom tomatoes have been selected and saved by generations of gardeners for their outstanding taste

Kitchen

Tomatoes are really fruits, but are most often used like vegetables in the kitchen. This distinction once caused such confusion that in 1893 the Supreme Court of the United States ruled that the tomato be reclassified as an official vegetable, even though in botanical terms it isn't.

Heirloom tomatoes, with their many colours, flavours and textures, are incredibly versatile—from big, flavoursome varieties that are perfect for stuffing, to types suitable for drying or for using in fresh salads and sauces. They look gorgeous all tossed together in a bowl. Follow the lead of creative chefs and experiment with new and exciting ways to use heirloom tomatoes.

BASIL

In the kitchen, sweet basil and tomatoes are natural companions. It's also one of the main ingredients in pesto, along with olive oil and pine nuts. It is a summer herb that can be grown from seed or seedlings in spring. Grow it in pots by a light window or in a sunny spot in the herb garden. Basil likes warm weather, so plant seedlings out when there is no risk of frost and you'll have fresh garden-picked basil throughout the warmer months. The most common kind has soft dark green leaves, but there are lime green, purple and ruffled varieties available.

My favourite varieties

There are so many varieties of heirloom tomatoes to choose from. What you select will depend on your conditions, the particular taste that appeals to you and how you wish to serve them. Here's some you could try:

Tommy Toe is the best one for my money! It has loads of 6-centimetre red or yellow fruit with an outstanding sweet flavour, and crops for about five months. In my house they rarely make it to the salad bowl because they're so irresistible picked from the vine. They're also delicious dried or when made into paste.

Green Zebra is tops for its slightly acidic taste and high yield, providing a steady crop of exquisitely striped, fleshy fruit for up to four months. What's more, birds don't find the fruit attractive. They are ready to pick when the fruit is striped green and yellow.

Black Russian has a nice crop of firm, medium-sized fruit with unusual charcoal-coloured flesh. These tomatoes have a lovely rich, sweet taste and are very fleshy. They are great in salads or served dried, and are ideal for sauces. They fruit for about four months.

Broad Ripple Yellow Currant produces tiny, bite-sized yellow fruits that are deliciously sweet and ideal for salads. Yielding large crops, the vines last into winter in many regions. These tomatoes are the perfect size for eating straight out of the garden. Delicious!

Tigerella lives up to its name with wonderfully decorative tomatoes that sport red and yellow stripes. The plant produces loads of small, round fruit, ideal for salads and tomato paste. This early variety appears in many regions from mid-June until September.

Jaune Flammee is a small tomato that's big on taste. Its fruit has brilliant orange skin that covers blushed yellow-red flesh. A wonderfully decorative plant, this meaty old French variety is a joy to cut into. With its explosive flavour, it's a good tomato for drying.

White Snowball produces unusual medium-sized white fruit with few seeds. This meaty but sweet tomato is not as acidic as most and was traditionally used to make preserves. A late-season variety, it produces fruit right up to winter in temperate climates.

Speckled Roman is a decorative Roman-style tomato. These elongated tomatoes are scarlet red with distinctive wavy yellow stripes. With a very sweet, rich flavour, these medium-sized tomatoes are ideal for making pastes.

Tomato tart tatin

Serves 6

Balsamic reduction

1 cup balsamic vinegar

⅓ cup caster sugar

1. Combine balsamic vinegar and sugar
in a saucepan on the stove, stirring until
sugar dissolves. Reduce by half, then
remove from heat and allow to cool.

Tart tatin

250 g cherry tomatoes

1 sheet puff pastry

1. Halve the cherry tomatoes and season
with salt and pepper.
2. Line the bottoms of a six-cup muffin tin
with baking paper and place three to five
halved tomatoes, flesh side up, into each
muffin cup in the tin. Drizzle tomatoes with
the balsamic reduction.
3. Cut the puff pastry into discs to match
the size of the muffin cups, and place discs
on top of the tomatoes, pushing the sides
down into the tin.
4. Bake for 15–20 minutes at 180°C.
5. Turn out and serve with pastry side down.

Heronswood tomato salad

Serves 4

1 kg Greek-style yoghurt
  (to make labna, a yoghurt cheese)
500 g assorted heirloom tomatoes,
  the more variety in colour and
  size the better
8 torn basil leaves
4 sprigs fresh thyme
6 black peppercorns
2 peeled garlic cloves
Vinaigrette (see page 189)

1. To make the labna, take 1 kg of Greek-style yoghurt, place in a muslin-lined sieve or colander and position over a bowl to drain.

2. Place a saucer on top of the yoghurt along with a 500 g weight and place in the refrigerator overnight in order to press out as much liquid as possible. Discard the liquid from the bowl the next morning and roll the labna into walnut-sized balls.

3. Place the balls in a wide-mouthed jar filled with good olive oil, and add the fresh thyme sprigs, peppercorns and garlic to the oil. Stored in the fridge, the labna will keep for one week.

4. To assemble salad, quarter or slice the larger tomatoes but leave the small ones whole. Place in a bowl, add the vinaigrette and torn basil leaves and toss so that the tomatoes are well coated.

5. Transfer the tomato mixture into the salad bowl and top with labna. Drizzle a little extra oil from the labna jar, and season with salt and pepper to taste.

Confit of truss tomatoes

Serves 4 as a side dish

4 tomato trusses,
  preferably Sugar Lump tomatoes
500 ml (approx.) olive oil
2 cloves garlic
2 sprigs rosemary
5 peppercorns
1 bay leaf

1. Pour enough oil into a small saucepan to eventually cover the truss when it's later added.
2. Add the garlic, rosemary, peppercorns and bay leaf to the oil and gently heat to approximately 70°C (around the temperature of hot tap water). Allow the flavours to infuse for about 15 minutes.
3. Submerge the truss in the oil while maintaining heat, until the tomatoes are softened, being careful not to split the skin. Drain.
4. The oil can be reserved and used later in cooking.

Oven-roasted tomatoes

Serves 6 as a side dish

1 kg roma-style tomatoes
Salt and ground pepper
Extra-virgin olive oil

1. Cut tomatoes lengthwise and place
onto a wire cake rack in a roasting pan,
with sliced side facing up. Sprinkle
tomatoes with salt and freshly ground
pepper, then drizzle with olive oil.
2. Place into a warm oven and cook at
130°C for approximately 45 minutes
or until desired amount of drying is
achieved.

Beans

Common beans (*Phaseolus vulgaris*), also known as French beans, are frost-tender annuals. Among them are both climbing and dwarf (bush) forms. Some gardeners find the climbing varieties messy and demanding in terms of space, but they are superior in productivity to the dwarf types and, when trained up tripods and along trellises, bring the added dimension of height to the garden. Dwarf varieties haven't the vigour or productivity of climbing types, but their crop matures earlier and they have a neat habit, which makes them ideal for small gardens or containers on the patio.

There are beans with green, purple, yellow, and striped or flecked pods that are incredibly beautiful, and ensure you look like a gourmet cook every time you serve them. Pod shape also varies from wide flat pods, like the heirloom Italian Romano, to long pencil-thin pods seen in varieties of other species like the snake bean. Then there are the yellow wax-pods, or butter beans, which have a dull, waxy appearance. Another point to look out for is whether they are stringless, a trait which makes them tender and easy to prepare. The most sought-after varieties are those which combine good flowers and flavour, such as the heirloom Purple King with pretty purple blooms and pods that turn green when cooked, as well as tasty, productive varieties like Lazy Housewife's Bean, which used to be a rarity but is now more widely available.

Runner beans (*Phaseolus coccineus*) are ideal if you live in a cooler area and enjoy mild summers. They are perennial plants which retreat underground in winter and grow from the crown again the following spring. The flattish pods are most tender when picked young (about 10–12 cm long), and can be cooked and served whole, or left to ripen and dry on the plant so that the seeds can either be removed and stored for use in winter soups or replanted the following season. Most varieties climb to 3 metres or more, but there are also less productive dwarf types. Runner beans produce attractive flowers, the best being the red-flowered Scarlet Runner.

Health and nutrition

Although each variety may vary in composition, beans are generally a great source of vegetable protein and are rich in iron, making them an excellent option for vegetarians. They also contain vitamins A and C, B-group vitamins, calcium, potassium and folic acid, and are a good source of zinc— an important element in a range of enzymes that support body functions such as digestion and

metabolism. Beans also provide large amounts of soluble fibre, which helps to lower cholesterol and maintain a healthy digestive system.

Growing

Beans are easily grown in warm, sunny positions in most soils, provided regular water is available. They prefer a more neutral soil and benefit from the addition of lime or dolomite if the soil is too acidic. Climbing varieties in particular dislike strong winds, so they appreciate a sheltered spot.

Beans are frost-tender plants and most are grown as annuals. It is best to wait until soils have warmed and the risk of frost has passed before sowing seeds. Alternatively, sow seeds indoors or under glass. Climbing beans can be trained to grow up a trellis, fence or frame, or up a wigwam or tripod of garden stakes. Position climbing types 10–20 centimetres apart. Once they start growing, help plants to cling on by directing them up the climbing support. Unlike climbing types, dwarf beans need no support and can be sown in rows 10 centimetres apart or in random patterns at 30-centimetre spacing.

Slugs and snails find young beans very appetising, so protect the emerging seedlings with a barrier of sharp grit, snail traps or animal-friendly pellets—and watch out for foraging birds. Once flowering commences give plants a regular dose of a liquid food. Beans have shallow root systems so be careful not to disturb the roots too much when weeding.

CROP ROTATION
Beans are members of the Leguminosae
family and are able to produce their own
soil nitrogen via the nodules in the
legume roots, so are best followed by
nitrogen-greedy brassica crops.

Harvest

Dwarf, or bush beans, generally mature faster than climbing varieties and can be harvested eight to ten weeks after sowing. More productive climbing types may take up to three months to fully ripen.

You can pick the immature pods every three to five days in the height of the season and cook them whole as a side dish, or use them in salads. When the last beans are ready to harvest you can leave some on the plant to dry, both for storage through winter (the dried beans of many varieties can be used in soups or soaked in water before they are cooked) and to sow as seed the following year.

Kitchen

Beans are a classic side dish and make a great addition to summer salads. Decorative varieties like Rattlesnake don't tend to keep their colour or pattern when cooked, but some of the visual effect may be preserved by a light blanching only (for me, light cooking is the best approach with any bean, helping to retain their full flavour and crunch). Dried bean seeds are a great cupboard standby for winter soups.

My favourite varieties

Lazy Housewife's Bean got its old-fashioned name because of its incredible yields and the way its beans grow in clusters, so they're easy to pick. There's no doubt as to the value of this stringless variety, which has been cultivated in gardens for nearly two centuries. It is a late-season climbing variety, producing an abundance of thick, fleshy beans 12–15 centimetres long, perfect for cooking or picking and eating fresh. Although not widely available, it is well worth looking for.

Rattlesnake is a climbing variety which produces deep green beans splashed with purple, over a long season. It tops the list for taste and is appropriately named for its seeds, whose decorative markings resemble those on a rattlesnake. Seeds can be sown after the risk of frost is over. It's harder to track down, but worth seeking out for its incredible flavour, pretty pink and mauve flowers and high yields. It flowers and fruits for up to four months and is delicious cooked or eaten raw.

Dragon's Tongue is a bush variety that produces long finger-like beans on a compact plant just 60 centimetres tall. The waxy, plump yellow pods are stringless and have decorative purple streaks that vanish when they are cooked. These crisp, juicy beans are delicious eaten whole or dried and stored for winter soups.

Purple King displays purple flowers and pods, which hang like fingers from the vine and are incredibly decorative. This climbing variety is at its best trained up stakes or wigwams in the kitchen or flower garden. The purple pods are deliciously tender but lose their intense purple colour when cooked.

Scarlet Runner is so named for its brilliant scarlet flowers and climbing habit, and is worth growing purely for its looks—although it does taste good too. The pods are wide and flat, and contain decorative purple seeds with black speckles. It's a perennial which dies back over winter and re-emerges each spring. For best results replace plants every four to five years. Grow Scarlet Runner up wigwams or willow poles, surrounded by other vegetables and flowers.

Beans with toasted almonds and burnt butter

Serves 4

300 g Blue Lake or other green beans
80 g whole almonds, crushed into chunks
50 g butter
150 g cherry tomatoes, halved
Salt and pepper, to taste

1. Quickly blanch the beans in boiling salted water for two minutes, and then refresh in cold water and drain.
2. Heat the butter in a pan until it starts to foam, then add the crushed almonds and stir until brown. Add the beans and tomatoes and toss until they are warmed through. Season with salt and pepper.

Salad of Purple King beans

Serves 4

400 g Purple King beans
250 g cherry tomatoes
30 ml vinaigrette (see page 189)
Salt and pepper, to taste

1. Top and tail the beans, and blanch for two minutes in salted boiling water. Refresh beans in cold water and drain.
2. Slice the beans into diagonal julienne strips and place in a mixing bowl along with the tomatoes.
3. Toss with the vinaigrette, and season with salt and pepper.

Recipes

Apples

Native to temperate Europe and Asia, apples (*Malus domestica*) have been cultivated for thousands of years. With their glossy skin, tasty flesh and versatility in the kitchen, they remain a tempting favourite throughout the world.

Since the beginning of the 20th century the number of cultivars of apples available has dropped substantially. Sadly many of the old varieties are difficult to find today, replaced by a handful of varieties which meet the commercial imperative for uniform, blemish-free fruit. Some of the apples that our grandparents treasured have faded into obscurity and the effort to save these varieties is a race against the clock.

There's something thrilling about hunting down these 'lost' varieties and growing 'antique' apples in your own garden. By antique, I don't mean apples that have been sitting in the fruit bowl too long. I'm talking about those old varieties that were well known 100 years ago. They have curious names like Pig's Nose Pippin, Bloody Ploughman and Duck's Bill, each with specific uses in the kitchen. Part of the appeal of antique apples is some of the interesting flavours and aromas they possess, such as the strawberry-flavoured Tydeman's Early Worcester, the honey tasting Sweet Bough and the delightful Esopus Spitzenberg, which smells like cinnamon when cut.

I'm horrified to think that many people's only experience of apples is confined to the half-dozen or so choices you find at the supermarket, particularly when you can grow such an astounding variety of apples, all with different colours, flavours and textures. I'd much rather a tasty apple with a few spots than perfect looking fruit without flavour!

DID YOU KNOW...

Isaac Newton was inspired to create his theory of universal gravitation by observing an apple fall in an orchard. A supposed descendant of Newton's apple tree can be found growing in the Botanic Gardens in Cambridge, England, and there are also alleged clones of the original tree in Australia.

Health and nutrition

Apples are considered to be an important food for the promotion of good health—as they say, 'An apple a day keeps the doctor away'. Apples are a good source of immune-boosting vitamin C and are abundant in quercetin, a flavonoid linked to the prevention of certain cancers and also believed to have antihistamine properties that reduce the symptoms of allergies. Apples are also an excellent source of the dietary fibre pectin, which helps to lower cholesterol, maintain blood sugar levels and relieve digestive complaints. If you haven't got a toothbrush handy, eating an apple is a good substitute. They are said to cleanse the mouth of large amounts of the bacteria that cause tooth decay.

SPACE-SAVING TIPS

While some varieties of cultivated apple can grow up to 15 metres tall, many antique apples have been grafted onto dwarf rootstock, which restricts their height to between 2 and 3 metres. Dwarf rootstock can also trick the variety into fruiting around two years earlier than they would if grafted onto a taller rootstock. Apples are tolerant of heavy pruning, so in a small garden they can be espaliered to fit narrow areas. Some of the dwarf varieties will also perform well in large pots.

Growing

There are apple varieties that suit most climates, but they generally perform best in cool and temperate regions, with most varieties being tolerant to frost. Apples are mostly small-spreading trees that fit neatly into a sunny spot in the garden and give months of pleasure with their pretty blossom and tasty fruit. In fact, you can have apples on your trees from July through to November, depending on whether they are early-, mid- or late-fruiting varieties.

Apple trees can be planted bare-rooted in winter when they are dormant, before spring growth starts. They tolerate part shade but grow best in full sun. They also like to have protection from fierce winds. The soil should be fertile and well drained, so incorporate plenty of compost before planting your tree. As a rule, apples need a good supply of water, especially in spring and summer.

Mulch the tree with a layer of straw and well-rotted compost or blood and bone and feed it with a complete fertiliser in early spring. Apples generally like a soil pH in the range of 6–7, so most soils benefit from an application of lime or wood ash every spring.

Annual pruning is important to ensure a good crop and establish a strong framework of branches. The pruning technique depends on the variety and vigour of the rootstock, so ask for pruning advice.

Remove grass growing around the base of your trees to reduce the competition for water and nutrients. Consider planting perennial vegetables and herbs—these make good companions—as well as flowering plants and shrubs, which attract friendly pollinators. If you have chickens, let them roam around trees so they can feed off the larvae of codling and light brown apple moths.

Some fruit trees, such as peaches and nectarines, are self-fertile, meaning one tree alone will produce a good crop. Nearly all apples, however, require a pollinating partner to be planted close by in order to produce bountiful fruit. Each variety has various partners that are compatible, which may vary from area to area, so ask your local nursery for advice. As a general rule, a suitable pollinating partner is one that flowers at the same time, allowing the pollen from one variety to be transferred to the stigma of another—this is known as cross-pollination. If you don't know what type of apples you've got in the garden, try planting a Jonathan, which will pollinate most other varieties as well as itself.

If you live in an older suburb you may not need a pollinating partner at all. It's likely that there are apple trees growing in your area, even a couple of kilometres away, that are capable of pollinating your trees—with the help of bees, of course.

OTHER POLLINATING IDEAS
When your tree is in bloom you could put a flowering branch from
a friend's tree into a plastic bottle filled with water and hang it from
a branch to aid pollination. Some people even graft a branch
from a compatible pollinating variety onto their tree.

Harvest

It's best to pick apples when they reach maturity. If you leave them hanging on the tree too long they can become floury or taste bitter. Harvest green apples when the background colour is pale green or yellow, and pick red ones when they start to turn a deeper red.

RIPE TO EAT
Apples may be described as early, mid or late—this refers to the
ripening times. Though these times vary with climate and altitude,
here's a general guide to when they ripen:

Early varieties—July to September.
Mid varieties—October to December.
Late varieties—January to April.

Kitchen

There are more ways to eat apples than straight off the tree. They are incredibly versatile in the kitchen and can be used for juice, jelly, cider, sauce, butter, baking, stewing, drying, brandy, vinegar, preserves and pastries. Each variety may be more suited to a particular purpose, so check labels and talk to your nursery or orchardist to help select the best varieties for you.

Apples store well under the right conditions and as a result can be eaten fresh throughout most of the year. Undamaged apples can be stored for months with their stalks left on in a cool, dark area with good air circulation and where they're protected from rodents. Place them in a wooden crate padded with dry straw. You can also dry, or puree and freeze them for year-round use.

My favourite varieties

Many of these antique varieties are hard to source, but worth the effort. Track down heritage fruit groups in your area for advice on where to get them. These groups may also have lots of other suggestions for good varieties suitable for your garden.

Cox's Orange Pippin is a popular English variety and is the tastiest dessert apple. Its sweet, dense yellow flesh is delicious eaten fresh but the apple is also good in pies or juiced. This upright, moderately vigorous tree performs best in areas with cool summers. Golden Delicious and *Pomme de Neige* are good pollinators. A mid-season variety that lasts well on the tree.

Bramley's Seedling originated in England in 1809. This vigorous spreading tree bears a heavy crop of big green-yellow apples with red-brown stripes. Its slightly acidic flesh is good in pies, stewed or juiced. Good pollinators for this triploid variety are Golden Delicious, Jonathan and Idared. This variety ripens late in the season.

Mutsu was developed in 1937 in Japan, where it sold for such high prices it was called the million-dollar apple. Its large fruit, green-yellow skin, spicy honey taste and juicy flesh is good for cider and desserts. Granny Smith and Jonathan are good pollinators for this late variety.

Fox Whelp is known as a 'bittersharp' apple that makes fantastic cider. It was thought to have been found in the 17th century near a fox's den in Gloucester. This moderately vigorous tree produces a good crop of dusky red fruit. Sweet Coppin, Egremont, Russet, Yarlington Mill and *Fameuse* all make good pollinators. This variety ripens early in the season.

Pine Golden Pippin is a dessert apple that originated in England in 1861. This moderately vigorous tree has an upright spreading habit and produces small fruit with rusty looking skin and tasty, almost pineapple-flavoured flesh. Braeburn, Rome Beauty, Northern Spy and Golden Delicious are ideal pollinators. It ripens late in the season.

Opalescent tops my list of great eating apples. This moderately vigorous, upright spreading tree bears large red fruit with bright skin. It's delicious eaten straight from the tree but also keeps well. Advance (Laxton's), Allen's Everlasting, Granny Smith and Allington Pippin make good pollinating partners. It is a mid-season variety.

Maigold is a good eating apple that was raised in Switzerland in 1964. This vigorous, slightly weeping tree bears sweet, crisp yellow fruit. The flesh has a honey flavour that develops a citrus tang as it ripens. Most early to mid varieties, such as Granny Smith, make good pollinators. It is a late season variety.

London Pippin (Five Crown) originated in England in 1831. It's great for making cider, cooking, drying and eating fresh. This moderately vigorous, upright spreading tree bears medium-sized yellow fruit. Red Delicious, Baxter's Pearmain and Golden Delicious are all suitable pollinators. This variety ripens late in the season.

Baked apples

Serves 4

4 cooking apples, cored

Filling

60 g pistachio nuts, shelled,
  toasted and coarsely crushed

60 g butter, softened

30 g caster sugar

1. Mix the filling ingredients together
to make a firm compound.

2. Stuff the core cavity of the apples with
the compound and place apples onto an oven
tray lined with baking paper.

3. Bake at 180°C until apple is tender
(approximately 25 minutes).

4. Serve with fresh double cream.

Apple tart

Serves 8

4 cooking apples

1 tablespoon lemon juice

Batter

10 tablespoons self-raising flour

6 tablespoons caster sugar

8 tablespoons milk

2 eggs

4 tablespoons sunflower oil

1 teapoon vanilla essence

Pinch of salt

Topping

60 g butter, softened

Caster sugar, extra

1. Peel, core and slice the apples, then sprinkle
both sides with lemon juice.

2. Place batter ingredients in a blender and
process until smooth and well mixed.

3. Grease and line a 25-cm flan tin with baking
paper. Pour the batter mixture into the flan tin
and arrange the apple slices in a fan shape on
top of the batter.

4. Dot the apple slices with butter and extra
caster sugar. Bake at 200°C for 25 minutes or
until the tart rises and turns golden brown.

5. Sift icing sugar on top and serve with
a generous dollop of pure cream.

Peaches

You know you're eating a good peach (*Prunus persica*) when the flesh is as sugary as any dessert and the juice runs freely down your chin and hands until you're a sticky mess. For me nothing can match the sweetness and flavour of a tree-ripened peach. There is something wonderfully child-like about sitting under a peach tree sampling the ripe fruit until you just can't eat any more.

Peaches grow on small deciduous trees so they're a good choice for the home garden, even if space is limited. Traditionally grown in glasshouses, peaches also perform well in warm, sheltered sites, such as against a sunny wall. Peaches are largely self-fertile, producing fruit on their own, with a few exceptions such as the yellow-fleshed J.H. Hale which requires a pollinating partner.

Peaches generally ripen from May to October, depending on the variety and the season. I have a fondness for sweet, white-fleshed peaches like the Australian variety Red Noonan, with its soft juicy texture. Yellow-fleshed varieties such as Golden Queen are just as tempting. Golden Queen ripens late in the season—around September in most climates—and has firm tasty flesh, so it's ideal for preserving.

There are both freestone and clingstone peach varieties. Golden Queen is an example of a clingstone peach, meaning that the seed doesn't fall away from the flesh when you pull the fruit apart, so you have to eat around the stone or cut it out with a knife. Clingstones have firmer flesh and retain their shape and colour better than freestones, so they're ideal for canning and bottling. With freestone peaches like Red Noonan, the stone falls away from the flesh and they have a softer, melt-in-your-mouth texture. Peaches can also be categorised by shape, and may be described as oblong, ovate, rounded or slightly flat.

Health and nutrition

Peaches are a rich source of vitamin C, iron and potassium. They are low in kilojoules and may have a gentle laxative effect. They have long been linked to longevity in the Chinese Taoist philosophy—in fact, the word 'tao' means peach. Their fruit, leaves, bark and seeds have been used in Chinese medicine for thousands of years for the treatment of a variety of ailments. Modern studies have linked the phytochemicals in peaches to the inhibition of tumour growth and microbial activity. Peaches are common as canned produce, but fresh is definitely best. The canning process is believed to result in a loss of about 80 per cent of the vitamin C content.

Growing

Although peach trees are easy to grow, they do prefer humus-rich, well-drained soil and full sun. Sun brings colour to the skin of the fruit, and in my experience the redder the blush, the sweeter the flesh. In city gardens peach trees can be fan- or herringbone-trained against a sunny courtyard wall.

Don't expect fruiting for the first couple of years after planting, but after that crops should be plentiful. By late spring lots of small green peaches appear on the branches. It is important to thin out your crop to ensure healthy good-sized fruit. This process can be a little disheartening, especially when you are sacrificing more fruit than you are keeping, but the rewards are worth it. When the fruit is roughly the size of a hazelnut, gently lift and twist off the young peaches, leaving just one or two fruits per cluster. You may need to thin again in early summer, until the fruit is roughly 15–20 centimetres apart.

Peaches flower and fruit mainly on wood grown in the previous summer. Winter pruning removes those branches which produced fruit last season and encourages fruiting wood for the next crop.

PREVENTION IS BETTER THAN CURE

Peach leaf curl (fungal disease) can pose a big problem, resulting in twisted, blistered leaves and leaf fall. A preventative fungicide applied in late winter just before the buds break is the best defence.

Harvest

Peaches should start to ripen by summer, depending on the variety. Birds love ripe peaches, so consider netting your trees. To test whether a peach is ripe, hold the fruit gently in your hand and press lightly close to the stalk. If it feels tender, it's ready to harvest. Pick carefully so that you don't bruise the fruit.

Kitchen

Deliciously sweet, tree-ripened peaches are a dessert in themselves. They can be eaten with or without the furry skins. In most cases the ripe fruit peels easily, but a brief dunk in boiling water can help the process. Clingstone varieties with firm flesh are superb for bottling, so you can enjoy them throughout the year. Damaged fruit isn't a complete loss—the good bits are great stewed or baked in pies and tarts.

While peaches make scrumptious desserts and pastries, they are also great in chutneys and relishes to accompany more spicy or savoury dishes. Try pairing peaches with coriander, for instance, to make peach relish. Coriander adds flavour and aroma to a wide variety of Asian dishes, and can be direct-sown from seed in spring. The leaves, roots and seeds are all commonly used to flavour soups, salads and noodle dishes. The fresh roots are used in Thai dishes and coriander seed is used in many curry spice mixes. Harvest plants before they flower, when the leaves have the best flavour. Coriander can be frozen to use later, so you'll always have a fresh supply. In cooler regions, coriander enjoys an open, sunny position. It has a tendency to go to seed quickly in hot and dry summers, so in warmer regions choose a shaded area of the garden.

My favourite varieties

Golden Queen is a clingstone variety from New Zealand with yellow-orange skin. The deep orange flesh is firm and juicy, making it ideal for bottling and eating fresh. It bears a heavy crop late in the season.

J.H. Hale is a red-skinned, yellow-fleshed peach that ripens around July to September, and is delicious picked and eaten fresh. While peaches are generally self-fertile, the freestone J.H. Hale is the exception to the rule, requiring another variety to fertilise its flowers.

Summerset is a valuable late-season freestone variety, which ripens in September. The fruit is large with attractive red skin and firm yellow flesh, so it's excellent for bottling, drying or eating fresh.

Tasty Zee is a delicious late-season freestone peach with dark red skin and firm, juicy, sweet white flesh. It can be dried, but is best eaten straight from the tree. I've written a lot about the virtues of older varieties, but Tasty Zees are a reminder that there are some wonderful new varieties that are full of flavour.

Daisy is firm and juicy with beautifully flavoured white flesh and creamy red-blushed skin. It's a newer freestone cultivar, which produces a prolific crop of fruit mid-season. Trees grow to around 4 metres tall.

Peach relish

8 ripe freestone peaches,
  peeled and coarsely chopped
¼ bunch coriander, chopped
4 spring onions
1 lemon, zest and juice
1 tablespoon brown sugar
1 chilli, finely diced

1. Combine all the ingredients and let stand for 30 minutes.
2. Serve with grilled or pan-fried salmon, chicken, veal or pork.

Gratin of peach with Muscat sabayon

Serves 4

2 cups water
2 cups sugar
4 white-fleshed peaches
Sabayon
150 g caster sugar
6 egg yolks
70 ml Muscat

1. Combine the water and sugar in a large saucepan. Stir over medium low heat without boiling until the sugar has completely dissolved. Bring just to the boil then add the peaches. Reduce the heat and simmer for 10 minutes. Using a slotted spoon, lift the peaches from the syrup, and place onto a plate to cool slightly. Slip off the skins.
2. To make the sabayon, put the sugar and egg yolks into a heatproof bowl and place onto a saucepan of barely simmering water. Don't let the bottom of the bowl touch the water. Using electric beaters or a whisk, beat until the mixture is pale and creamy. Add the Muscat and keep whisking for about 10 minutes, until thick and increased in volume.
3. Place the peaches into a shallow heatproof dish. Pour the sabayon over the peaches and cook carefully under a hot grill for 30 seconds, or until lightly coloured.

Freestone peach tart

Serves 8

4 freestone peaches

Sweet pastry

500 g plain flour
Pinch of salt
250 g unsalted butter
2 eggs, 100 g caster sugar and
  1 tablespoon water, beaten together

Crème patisserie

6 egg yolks
125 g caster sugar
1 tablespoon butter
¼ teaspoon vanilla essence
60 g plain flour
500 ml milk

1. To make the pastry, sift the flour and salt into a basin, and rub in butter to resemble breadcrumbs. Make a well in the centre and add the egg mixture, combining the ingredients into a smooth paste. Do not overwork. Cover, refrigerate and allow to rest for at least 30 minutes before using.

2. To make the créme patisserie, cream the yolks, sugar, butter and vanilla essence together, add flour and beat mixture thoroughly to form a smooth paste.

3. Place the mixture in a saucepan and bring to the boil. Add half the milk to the mixture, whisking vigorously until smooth, then whisk in the remaining milk. Remove from heat.

4. Roll out the pastry, press it into a 20-cm loose-bottomed flan tin and bake it for 20 minutes at 170°C. While the pastry is baking, cut the peaches in half, remove the stones and thinly slice the flesh into segments.

5. Remove the pastry from the oven, fill the case with the crème patisserie and place the sliced peach on top in a fan arrangement. Dust the tart with icing sugar and place under the grill for a few minute or until the icing sugar is slightly browned. Serve with a generous dollop of double cream.

Berries

I remember sitting out in the garden as a child greedily eating all the berries I could stomach. Every time I have to buy a punnet I find myself wishing for the delicious sweetness that only garden-fresh berries can provide—so sweet that it would be sinful to sprinkle them with sugar! Berries perish quickly—a perfect excuse to eat them straight from the plant. Be sure to plant twice what you need because they have the mysterious habit of disappearing on the way to the kitchen.

Health and nutrition

They may be small, but berries really pack a punch when it comes to health benefits. Researchers from the USDA Human Nutrition Centre rank blueberries as number one for antioxidant capacity, ahead of 40 other fresh fruits and vegetables. They have been linked to protection against cancers, heart disease, strokes and urinary tract infections, and various studies have shown their potential for reversing age-related impairment in memory and muscle coordination.

Blueberries are a good source of vitamins A and C, zinc, potassium, iron, calcium and magnesium, and contain the phytochemical lutein, which is linked to healthy vision. They are also high in fibre and low in kilojoules.

Strawberries come second to blueberries for antioxidant capacity and contain various phytochemicals that have been shown to fight carcinogens and protect against heart disease. They contain more vitamin C than any other berry and are a good source of folic acid, manganese, potassium and fibre.

Raspberries are also rich in cancer-fighting phytochemicals and are a good source of vitamins A, C and E, calcium and folic acid. They also contain soluble fibre in the form of pectin, which helps to lower cholesterol and maintain a healthy digestive tract.

Growing

STRAWBERRIES

Good drainage and full sun is vital for strawberries. Where drainage is a problem, grow them in raised beds or in pots and hanging baskets on your patio or balcony. This is also a good option for deterring slugs and snails, which enjoy strawberries as much as we do!

Before planting, prepare the soil with compost and organic matter. Mulch generously to conserve

moisture and suppress weeds. Straw is a good choice because it also provides a clean bed for the ripe berries.

It's a good idea to top up beds with compost or well-rotted manure each year, and apply a liquid fertiliser every three weeks or so after flowering commences to promote a healthy crop.

TREAT YOURSELF...

There are lots of firm-fleshed commercial varieties of strawberries available, bred more for durability than flavour. For a real treat try growing some of the heirloom varieties with succulent flesh and vastly superior flavours and aromas.

BLUEBERRIES

Blueberries are bursting with sweetness and have a delectable texture that explodes on your tongue. They are largely deciduous plants that lose their leaves in autumn, although some varieties will maintain their foliage. In spring they display pink or white flowers which develop into sumptuous summer berries, and many have attractive autumn foliage.

Blueberries grow best in well-drained acidic soil—somewhere in the pH range of 4.5 to 5.5 is ideal—in either full sun or part shade. They enjoy cool winters, which promote the development of flower buds, but protect them from late frost. Some varieties perform well in warmer regions, but they may need to be grown in more shaded areas. They are wonderfully productive plants that can produce up to 4 kilos of berries each season. A regular liquid feed will give them a real boost.

RASPBERRIES

I would grow raspberries just so I could enjoy them fresh and smothered in thick dollops of cream.

Raspberries are traditional summer bearers, which flower and fruit on the canes they made in the previous year, but there are also varieties that crop in autumn on the current season's growth and other dual croppers that do both.

All raspberries have a suckering habit, so grow them as a hedgerow or in clumps a metre or so apart. Be sure to separate your varieties by a couple of metres because they will almost certainly grow together, and the stronger variety may overwhelm the weaker one as well as making pruning of the different types difficult. I always find it's better to plant them in a patch of their own because they have

a tendency to run rampant. You can bunch or tie canes up to make harvesting easier.

Raspberries enjoy a sunny site, but will grow in some shade. They love a rich soil, so refresh beds with compost each year and apply fertiliser in early spring to boost growth and fruiting. Like other berries, raspberries don't like to dry out, so keep the water up during hot spells, particularly once the fruit has started to form.

Harvest

Taste is the best guide for when to harvest your berries, so try a few each day and let your palate lead the way.

Pick strawberries when they are plump and ripe, so the sugar content is fully developed. Check them first for soft spots and mould. They are best picked and eaten straight away, but will keep for about 2–3 days in the refrigerator.

Harvest blueberries when they look plump and firm. The fruit should be dark in colour, so steer away from the red ones, which won't be ripe. You can keep blueberries for up to about 10 days in the refrigerator, or freeze and use as required over several months.

Raspberries are easily bruised, so harvest them carefully and pick out any berries that are crushed or bad. Pat them dry with a paper towel and devour them fresh or store them in a covered bowl in the refrigerator for about 3 days.

Kitchen

Berries are a particular favourite with kids and make delectable desserts, drinks, sauces and preserves. A bowl of fresh mixed berries, eaten with a rich dollop of full cream, is as spectacular to the eye as it is to the palate.

My favourite varieties

STRAWBERRIES

Cambridge Rival is deliciously sweet with a fragrance that calls you from every corner of the garden.

Chandler has a profusion of big red berries which are delicious picked fresh and served with ice-cream.

Hokowase is addictive eaten straight from the plant. I haven't tasted a sweeter strawberry.

Fraise des Bois, which produces tiny, sweet white fruit, is both unique and flavoursome, as is *Semper Florens*, with its tangy red or yellow fruit. Both are varieties of wild strawberries, which are especially tasty, providing hundreds of small intensely flavoured berries. Unlike the more common hybrids, wild strawberries, or 'bush alpines', belong to a non-running species that forms a bushy habit. The berries are also smaller and tarter, and the plants more vigorous. Best of all, you can replant the seeds.

BLUEBERRIES

Blue Rose produces sweet berries from June through to September on a bush about 2 metres tall.

Reveille is tops for taste, and has the bonus of pretty pink spring flowers and vibrant autumn foliage.

Northland can't be beaten for its several months of dark-fleshed, scrumptious berries. Leave the berries to ripen on the bush for the sweetest flavour. It is tolerant to extremes of both heat and cold.

RASPBERRIES

Willamette is a dual cropper with dark red fruit that has a wonderful flavour.

Neika is especially enticing, producing delicious, sweet berries in summer.

Heritage produces an autumn crop of small bright-red fruit on the current season's canes, and is also a variety I'm particularly fond of.

Fresh berries

Serves 4

250 g strawberries, hulled and halved

200 g blueberries

200 g raspberries

1 tablespoon caster sugar

125 ml freshly squeezed orange juice

1. Place all the berries into a shallow serving
bowl. Sprinkle the sugar over, and drizzle with
the juice.
2. Stand for 20 minutes, gently turning the
berries occasionally.
3. Serve with cream or good vanilla ice cream.

sweet peppers
and chillies

Sweet peppers, or capsicums as they are commonly known, are one of the most beautiful of fruits. With their colourful, shiny skins and unusual shapes, they are attractive as well as productive.

Peppers are members of the Solanaceae family, which also includes tomatoes and potatoes. Reflecting this, in cultivation they need similar conditions to tomatoes, although they do like a bit more heat. Peppers are native to Central and South America. In their native habitat they are perennial plants, but tend to be grown as annuals in gardens because of their sensitivity to frost.

While the ubiquitous green and red peppers are the most well known, there are more colours than you might realise. The immature fruit of most varieties is green, turning red, orange, yellow and even purple-black when ripe. The diversity of shape, too, is very broad, with block-shaped, square, squat, bell-shaped and long finger-like types, as well as some that twist like bulls' horns. The fruit itself can be thick or thin walled, and the plants upright or pendulous.

In the typical colour range of green-red my favourite is Chinese Giant. It's one of the superior older cultivars with wonderfully sweet bell-shaped peppers that ripen more ruby than red. Some of the more unusual coloured forms I like to grow include Orange Bell, Yellow Marconi, and the alluring Sweet Chocolate with glossy chocolate-brown skin and brown-red flesh. Mini sweet peppers such as Japanese Shishitou are especially delightful, with bite-sized fruit perfect for fresh summer salads.

Health and nutrition

Weight for weight, peppers contain more vitamin C than oranges and, along with beta-carotene and various phytochemicals, they provide considerable antioxidant effects, which are believed to help neutralise disease-causing free radicals and provide protection against cancers and other diseases. The hotter peppers, which we often refer to as chillies, are renowned in Chinese medicine for their capacity to improve the health and functioning of the respiratory system, including helping to clear congested sinus and nasal passages, and reducing the symptoms of asthma. They have also been linked to the prevention of stomach ulcers, the reduction of headaches, the lowering of blood cholesterol, the relief of inflammatory pain and assisting weight loss.

Growing

Fruiting crops like peppers need high temperatures to germinate. They are ideal for growing in greenhouses, in pots or beds, although warm, sheltered sites are also suitable. Like tomatoes, peppers are best grown in maximum sunlight. They can be direct-sown, but in cooler climates it is best to germinate them indoors or under glass and transplant them as seedlings, or buy them in punnets ready to plant out.

While peppers love the heat, they also enjoy regular, deep watering. It is also advisable to stake plants, particularly the bigger varieties, which are prone to snapping with the weight of the crop. Peppers have a deep root system, so before planting prepare the soil to a reasonable depth and incorporate organic matter. Peppers are also susceptible to the same soil pests and diseases as other members of the Solanaceae family, so avoid unwanted problems by adopting good crop rotation practices. Once the young peppers appear, fertilise weekly with a tomato food or complete fertiliser to encourage more fruit.

Harvest

Even if you don't like your peppers green, start harvesting some fruits once they are a decent size. This method seems to encourage additional flowers and fruit. The fruit of almost all varieties changes colour several times before reaching maturity. You can pick the immature fruit at any time if it is to your taste, but for the best flavour and highest vitamin C content, allow it ripen fully on the plant. Given the brittleness of the branches, I find it easier to harvest peppers with secateurs.

TOO HOT TO HANDLE...

Take particular care when handling the hot varieties. I wear heavy plastic gloves when harvesting and preparing them. My grandmother once spent an entire night with her hands in a bucket of water after chopping chillies without gloves.

My favourite varieties

Jimmy Nardello's Sweet Italian Pepper is generally classed as a frying variety, but it is one of the sweetest non-bell peppers I've ever tasted. It produces big yields of decorative bright red peppers that have a 'ram's horn' shape with thin walls and a somewhat wrinkled appearance. They can be harvested roughly 12–13 weeks from planting, when the peppers are around 16 centimetres long. Cooked or raw, they retain their sweet flavour.

Mini Chocolate is a delicious and succulent pepper, with Sweet Chocolate colour outside and brick-red colour inside. It is prolific and changes from green to brown as it matures. The bite-sized fruit is irresistible picked straight from the plant and tossed into salads. It's best eaten fresh because it is too small and fiddly to cook with.

Orange Bell stands out among the bell peppers for its superior flavour. It has lower yields and matures later in the season than most peppers, but the large sweet bells are worth the wait. The thick-walled, brightly coloured fruit is best eaten fresh and is a perfect addition to salads.

Yellow Marconi is a sweet Italian pepper that is traditionally a frying variety but is also delicious eaten fresh. The golden yellow fruit can grow up to a foot long and are ready to harvest 12–13 weeks from planting. Try them washed, sliced lengthways, rubbed in garlic-infused oil and chargrilled.

Hot chilli peppers

I have always enjoyed Asian and South American dishes laced with mouth-numbing hot chillies. It is somehow a pleasure to flush and sweat over a great meal. Chillies range in colour from yellow through to green, purple and red. When choosing which variety to grow, remember that chillies are rated one to ten according to how hot they are, ten being the hottest. Generally, the smaller the chilli the hotter it is, and watch out for the red ones, which are red-hot in colour and temperature.

Habenero Chilli is a bell-shaped fruit that is as hot as it gets, with intense heat and a strong tropical flavour. The chillies may be dark green to orange or red in colour.

Jamaican Bell Chilli is another top choice for chilli lovers. Its unusual shape makes it incredibly decorative. It is most popular in chutneys, curries and salsas.

Bird's Eye Chilli is small and intensely hot. It can be red or green, and is used often in Asian dishes.

Thai Hot Chilli is a long, thin fruit that is green to red in colour. It is popular in Asian cooking, and is mostly used whole because it is difficult to skin and seed.

Hungarian Cherry Pepper has wonderfully ornamental round fruit with varying heat. The green fruit is only mildly intense, but when it turns red it is fiery hot. It has a sweet flavour, so it is ideal for salads and pickles.

Serrano Chilli has bullet-shaped fruit with a strong hot flavour. The green fruit ripens to red, and is a good addition to salsas and sauces.

Banana Chilli is large and conical and can be red, yellow or green. It is only mildly hot and is often served stuffed or roasted.

Jalapeno is thick-fleshed and only mildly intense. It can be eaten when it is green or red to flavour anything from casseroles to burgers and burritos.

GET THAT CHILLI-PEPPER HIGH!

Eating hot chilli peppers may give you a thrill that is completely unexpected. Capsaicin, the hot stuff in chilli peppers, can induce a rush of endorphins in the brain that give you a pleasant 'high'. According to various studies, the capsaicin 'burns' the nerve endings of the tongue and mouth, sending pain signals to the brain. To protect the body from perceived injury, the brain secretes endorphins—natural painkillers—that bring about temporary feelings of pleasure and wellbeing. Another bite of the chilli triggers the release of more endorphins, and so on, building up into a delightful rush.

Pepper compote

3 red peppers

75 g demerara sugar

1 brown onion

50 ml red wine vinegar

50 g butter

1 teaspoon turmeric

1 teaspoon smoked paprika

1 teaspoon yellow mustard seeds

Ground pepper, to taste

1. Roughly chop the peppers and onions, then place all ingredients into a stainless steel saucepan.

2. Cover and cook slowly until tender, and then puree.

3. Serve as a dressing over seared veal, pork or chicken fillet.

Chilli oil

Makes 2 cups

500 ml olive oil

6 birds eye chillies, whole

4 cloves garlic, peeled

1. Place all the ingredients into saucepan and
gently heat until the oil begins to shimmer.
2. Remove from heat and allow to cool,
then pour into an airtight jar.
3. Stand for 1 week before using.

Pepper stack

Serves 2

2 red peppers

2 yellow peppers

Olive oil

250 g bocconcini cheese, cut into rounds

1 tablespoon pesto

1. Rub the peppers with a little olive oil
and roast whole on a baking tray for
10 minutes at 200°C or until skin is charred
and blistered. Cool and peel.
 2. Cut the peppers into thick strips. Using
one red and one yellow pepper, carefully
alternate three layers of cheese and coloured
pepper. Repeat for the second stack.
3. Place on an oven tray lined with baking
 paper and roast for 4 minutes at 180°C.
4. Drizzle with pesto to serve.

Corn

One of the fondest memories I have of travelling through parts of Asia is wandering through the lively street markets sampling fresh barbequed sweet corn. There's nothing like it. I still occasionally enjoy sweet corn roasted or barbequed, but more frequently steamed or boiled. While it is delicious with a touch of salty butter, it is one of the few vegetables that is immensely satisfying without seasoning.

A member of the grass family, corn is a common cereal crop. Long before commercial-scale production, corn was grown by the Native American Indians in order to make flour from the starchy cobs. They later cultivated sweeter varieties that became popular for eating fresh.

While those starchy types, which are ideal for making cornflour (such as maize), can still be grown (and dried and ground, if you can be bothered), it's the sweet corn varieties that most gardeners find space for. There are also popcorn varieties—some with interestingly coloured kernels—and a few, like Ornamental Indian Corn, whose cobs are largely decorative.

I think the test of good sweet corn is whether it can be eaten fresh without cooking, and this is certainly the case with heirloom varieties such as Golden Bantam and modern varieties like Breakthrough, whose deep yellow cobs can be consumed straight from the plant. As it grows, corn is incredibly majestic at the back of the border or kitchen garden. All corn has impressive statuesque foliage, although Variegated Corn has the added bonus of decorative striped white, green and pink leaves, making it a handsome plant in an ornamental garden setting.

Health and nutrition

Sweet corn is a good source of dietary fibre, carbohydrate, folic acid and iron. It also contains plenty of beta-carotene, a powerful antioxidant believed to protect the body against disease. Sweet corn also contains the phytochemical curcumin, another antioxidant that is considered to be anti-inflammatory in nature. Sweet corn is higher in kilojoules than most vegetables, but is a healthy option eaten fresh from the cob, or even dried and ground into cornmeal, which is a good alternative for those who experience sensitivity or allergy to wheat.

Growing

Corn is a warm-season crop that enjoys organically rich soil, so add some rotted manure and compost before planting. In cooler areas, you can begin sowing in late spring, after the risk of frost has passed, or sow seeds earlier in pots or punnets indoors or in a warm greenhouse. Planting is simple. The large seed (actually an individual kernel) can be simply sown by dropping it into a hole 2–3 centimetres deep.

Sweet corn is wind-pollinated, so plants rely on the wind to transfer pollen from one plant to another. Planting corn in a block (with 15–20 centimetres between plants), rather than rows, will assist pollination. Your chances are also better with a larger quantity of plants. While the tall plants don't stand up to really strong winds, some wind is important for pollination.

Corn should be given full sun and plenty of water if you can manage it, because it is shallow-rooted and therefore susceptible to drying out. This is particularly important from the time the 'tassels' (male flowers) appear on the tops of the stems until the cobs are swelling nicely. Liquid fertilisers are also beneficial throughout the growing season to encourage good cob development. Remove any weeds that appear, preferably by hand to avoid damaging the shallow roots, and rotate your crop each season to prevent the build up of soil-borne diseases. Also watch for hungry slugs and snails which can quickly demolish young seedlings. Caterpillars are the main problem during summer.

Sweet corn doesn't form a dense canopy, so I like to grow other low-growing crops beneath it to make the most of space and to help control weeds. This works well with cut-and-come-again vegetables such as lettuce, dwarf beans, trailing marrows and many of the leafy Asian greens. Just make sure they are on the sunny side of the bed to avoid shading from the corn.

Harvest

Corn needs between 90 and 150 days of growing time to mature, although timing will vary with variety and climate. To test for ripeness, strip away some of the green casing to reveal the cob and push your fingernail into a kernel. If the juice that spurts out is milky then the corn is ready to harvest. Clear fluid indicates the cob is under-ripe and needs a little more time to mature. When the silky threads at the end of the cob turn brown and dry out, it is another sign that the cobs are ready to harvest. To pick, simply support the stem and snap the cob off with a quick downward movement. Baby corn can be harvested from sweet corn varieties as young cobs 7–10 cm long.

Kitchen

There's nothing like the fresh smell of newly cut corn. It's one of those vegetables which tastes best eaten soon after harvesting, when it's at its sweetest. I enjoy it steamed and served with nothing but a dollop of butter and some cracked pepper, and it's also delectable when oven-baked or barbequed to perfection.

My favourite varieties

Ornamental Indian Corn is an excellent ornamental variety, popular for both garden and indoor decoration. The multicoloured cobs are a combination of cream, brown and red kernels. Hang the cobs to dry and use them for craft projects or make flour from the hard kernels. At 2.5 metres tall, it adds much-needed texture and height to your garden.

Honey and Cream Hybrid F1 doesn't just look good, it's sweet and succulent right to the core. It's a unique bi-coloured variety with super-sweet white and golden yellow kernels on the same cob. For best flavour, eat it within minutes of harvesting.

Golden Bantam is an heirloom variety which dates back to 1902. If you're after good old-fashioned sweet corn flavour then you can't go past this variety, with its golden yellow cobs and big starchy kernels that are full of flavour.

Corn fritters

Serves 6

100 g plain flour

175 g instant polenta

1/2 tsp bicarbonate soda

200 ml buttermilk

1 egg yolk

2 egg whites, stiffly beaten

200 g corn kernels

110 g creamed corn

1/2 red onion, diced

1 small Jimmy Nardello or other capsicum, diced

Butter, for pan-frying

1. Mix the flour, polenta, bicarbonate soda, buttermilk and egg yolk to form a batter. Fold in the corn kernels, creamed corn, onion and capsicum. When well combined, fold in the egg whites.

2. Melt some butter in a frypan and add the batter to the pan one tablespoon at a time in order to fry the individual fritters in batches. Gently fry each side until lightly golden, then remove from pan and drain on absorbent paper. Keep fritters warm until ready to serve.

3. Serve with a dollop of créme fraiche, or tzatziki (page 132) on the side.

Steamed corn with herb butter

Serves 4

4 cobs Breakthrough or other corn
125 g unsalted butter, softened
1 tablespoon fresh mixed herbs
  (thyme, oregano and parsley), finely chopped
1 teaspoon seeded mustard
Salt and pepper, to taste

1. Whip the butter in a mixer until it becomes pale, and then mix through the herbs, mustard and seasoning.
2. Bring a large pot of salted water to the boil, and cook the corn for 8 minutes. Drain and serve with the herb butter.

Beetroot

Many people claim to dislike beetroot, having only tasted the preserved variety and not the real thing. Fortunately, fresh garden-harvested beetroot is an altogether tastier experience than the vinegar-soaked canned version that most of us were raised on. Now that I know better, there's nothing quite like whole roasted baby beets or fresh beetroot grated raw on top of rocket and drizzled with olive oil.

The beets we eat today are actually the swollen root of the plant. The ancestor of beetroot dates back to prehistoric times when it grew wild along the seashores of Asia and Europe. At first, it was not recognised for its tasty roots, but rather the leafy greens. Even as beets spread through northern Europe they were primarily used for animal fodder, and it wasn't until the 16th century that they began to be valued as a root vegetable.

Aside from its intensely sweet flavour, another appealing thing about beetroot is the visual impact it has on the plate. It's one of a select number of vegetables that has the ability to turn a mundane looking dish into a feast for the eyes. I'm not just talking about the ordinary round purple beet that we are all familiar with, but the range of wonderful heirloom varieties that may be flat, cylindrical or tapered, and come in many shades of white, yellow and red. If you want to grow something visually spectacular, try Italian Chioggia, which has concentric rings of white and pink.

Sweet beets

Beetroot is low in kilojoules even though it has the highest sugar content of all vegetables.
In fact, in Europe the beet was often used as the raw material for the production of refined sugar.
Slower growing varieties such as Golden Beets often have the sweetest flavour.

Health and nutrition

Beetroot contains carotenoids and flavonoids, nutritional compounds thought to be powerful cancer-fighting agents, which have been particularly linked to the prevention of colon cancer. They are also high in the B vitamin, folate (folic acid), which studies have shown helps ward off lung cancer. Folic acid also plays an essential role in energy production, cell growth, nervous system functioning and the formation of red blood cells, and is particularly important for pregnant women to support the

development of a healthy foetus. Beets are also noted for their blood-detoxification and body-cleansing properties. The beetroot leaves are rich in calcium, essential for healthy teeth and bones, and are high in iron, which helps to maintain energy and carry oxygen around the body.

Growing

Beets are relatively simple to grow. They enjoy full sun but will grow in part shade, and like other root vegetables they need good drainage. Refresh the soil with well-rotted manure and compost before planting and, if necessary, create mounds to ensure the soil is free-draining. They do better in slightly alkaline to neutral conditions, so the addition of lime is beneficial in strongly acidic soils. Water regularly and apply a complete fertiliser during the growing season to ensure good root development.

There is a risk that beetroot will bolt if planted too early. I direct-sow beetroot seed from mid-spring to early autumn and harvest the beets roughly eight weeks later. Some gardeners plant beetroot later in the season to provide baby beets and leaves for picking through winter. Beetroot 'seed' is in fact a cluster of seeds, and you will need to thin the seedlings to about 8–10 cm apart in 30 cm rows (closer for baby beets) when they emerge.

Harvest

Beetroot can be harvested at different stages of maturity, but none are quite as delicious as baby beets, which can be pulled roughly six weeks after a spring sowing when they are about the size of golf balls. These young roots are like little packages of sweetness and are wonderful boiled or roasted whole. Beetroot is easily harvested with a gentle tug, as most of the root sticks up above the soil.

Kitchen

Wash any remaining soil from the root and twist the leaves off before cooking. Beets are best cooked whole and can be steamed, boiled or baked in foil. Cutting the beet before cooking causes the flesh to 'bleed' and lose the red juice that's so full of goodness. After cooking, the skin can easily be removed by hand (if preferred) and the beet served deliciously warm or left to cool. They can also be pickled or preserved for long storage.

The leafy tops of beetroot are edible and can be used in much the same way as spinach or silverbeet,

Golden Beets
9·12·05

adding colour and flavour to a variety of dishes. I enjoy them raw and tossed into salads, but they are also good cooked and seasoned as a side dish or added to quiches, soups and pastas.

THYME

Thyme (*Thymus vulgaris*) is popular in the kitchen for its highly aromatic foliage. It is commonly used to flavour soups, fish, meat, poultry and eggs, and is a feature in the recipe for 'Breast of organic chicken with Bull's Blood chard' included at the end of this chapter. There are dozens of thymes to choose from, with variations in flower and foliage colour. Thyme requires little attention once established and is one of those valuable herbs that will grow with little water. Plants can get straggly after a few years, so take some new cuttings every year as replacements. The creeping mat-like varieties are more difficult to harvest, but are wonderfully decorative, growing between paving slabs and as groundcover.

My favourite varieties

Italian Chioggia is as much a conversation piece as a thrill for the tastebuds. The orange-red skin is attractive, but the real surprise comes when you slice it down the middle, revealing concentric rings of pink and white flesh. It reminds me of those old-fashioned lollipops. The flesh is deliciously sweet and lovely roasted and served with crumbled Persian fetta. The leaves can also be steamed or used in salads.

Burpee's Golden has beets that are orange when harvested and turn a lovely rich golden yellow when cooked, providing great contrast to novelty types like Italian Chioggia. Golden beets are the sweetest and make delicious mini beets. The yellow-veined leaves are attractive in salads and the juice doesn't stain!

Mini Gourmet Beetroot are young beets harvested early to capture all their sweetness. Baby beets are popular in restaurants, and deservedly so as they are packed with flavour. Drizzle the beets with olive oil and bake them whole with fresh garlic. Serve with cream or as an accompaniment to white fish.

Bull's Blood has deep red roots that are deliciously sweet, but the real talking point is the blood-red foliage, or chard, which brings intense colour to the ornamental garden and the plate.

Breast of organic chicken with Bull's Blood chard

Serves 2

2 organic chicken breast fillets
Chard from Bull's Blood beetroots
1 tablespoon olive oil
4 sprigs of fresh thyme
60 ml dry white wine

1. Make a pocket by slicing lengthwise into the side of the chicken breast with a narrow-bladed knife.
2. Roll the chard into a cigar shape and carefully insert into chicken breast. In a hot frypan, heat a little olive oil and sear both sides of the chicken until lightly browned. Add the thyme and the white wine to the pan and cook for two minutes.
3. Place the chicken breasts and the remaining liquid into an ovenproof dish, and cook in a moderate oven for approximately 20 minutes until firm and lightly golden.
4. Carve the breasts crosswise into four slices and serve.

Roasted baby heirloom beetroot with Persian fetta

Serves 6

400 g heirloom beetroots such as Chioggia,
  Golden or Bull's Blood
100 g Persian fetta
50 ml vinaigrette (see page 189)
Salt and pepper, to taste

1. Trim the stalks off and rinse the beetroots, leaving the skin on.
2. Roast the whole beetroots in a moderate oven for approximately 60 minutes or until tender.
3. While hot, cut into quarters, season with salt and pepper, and toss with vinaigrette. Finish with crumbled Persian fetta.

Carrots

The carrot is a member of the Umbelliferae family and has feathery leaves like its relatives—parsley, dill and fennel. It's such a well-known vegetable, but we sometimes overlook its many virtues. Grown at home, carrots are one of those vegetables that increase ten-fold in flavour and are delicious raw or cooked in a variety of savoury or sweet dishes. It's also worth knowing that there is a lot more to this humble vegetable than the long orange carrots we're all familiar with. Gardeners can grow white, yellow, red and purple varieties, which bring exciting colour and intrigue to the plate.

Carrots come in a variety of shapes and sizes, including round- or stump-rooted, intermediate- and long-rooted types. I'm particularly fond of boutique varieties like purple-skinned carrots and the yellow-rooted Austrian Lobbericher, which is definitely a conversation piece around the dinner table. I also find varieties such as Mini Round irresistible. It has short, broad roots, a bit like a squashed golf ball, which make good use of the top soil and are particularly useful for heavy ground or for growing in containers.

Health and nutrition

As little as one carrot a day can have a range of health-promoting benefits. They are an abundant source of vitamins, minerals and enzymes—particularly beta-carotene which the body converts to vitamin A. This is essential for healthy eyes, especially night vision, explaining the age-old adage that carrots help you to see in the dark! Studies have shown that beta-carotene's powerful antioxidant properties also help to stimulate the body's immune system in the fight against infection and certain types of cancer. Carrots also contain dietary fibre, which is linked to the lowering of cholesterol and the maintenance of a healthy digestive system.

Growing

The most vital ingredient in growing carrots successfully is a light, well-drained soil. They dislike heavy, organically rich or compact soils, which impede root development. As with all root crops it is best to avoid a freshly manured plot, as the roots have a tendency to fork under nitrogen-rich conditions. Instead, enrich beds with a well-aged manure and compost or plant into beds that have previously grown a nitrogen-greedy crop like lettuce or cabbage. Carrots do best in soil with a pH range of 6.5 to 7.5. They also appreciate a consistent supply of water, to help prevent splitting.

Carrot seed is small and hard to sow thinly, so prepare the soil as finely as possible. The seeds can be direct-sown and thinned to 10 centimetres apart, or grown in seed-raising mix and transplanted as small seedlings, although I have found this method can result in forking or distortion of the roots. Be sure to keep beds devoid of weeds, which can easily overtake the young carrots. Being from a cool area, carrots can be sown from February onwards, and even earlier if covered with cloches or frames. It can take several weeks for the young seedlings to emerge. For a continuous supply, sow another row as soon as the first seedlings are through.

Harvest

Carrots usually reach maturity about three months after sowing, but can be pulled at any stage during the growing season. They are particularly sweet and tender harvested as baby carrots early in the season.

You can usually get a fair idea of a carrot's maturity by observing the size of the carrot top above the ground or by gently scraping away a bit of soil to check. In loose, friable soils, carrots can be easily pulled out. Where soils are heavier, loosen around them first with a fork.

Kitchen

The carrot's sweetness is second only to the beetroot, so they're a great raw snack and perfect for juicing, either on their own or in combination with beetroot, orange and ginger or your own concoction. They're also delectable roasted or slow cooked in soups and stews, and happen to be a key ingredient in one of my favourite treats—carrot cake. The leafy tops are also great freshly chopped and tossed into sauces, soups and salads.

Baby carrots (and miniature varieties) are best eaten straight from the garden, washed with their skins left unpeeled. They are magnificently sweet—an absolute favourite with the kids.

SAGE

In the kitchen, sage is the perfect complement to poultry and pork.
It combines well with other strongly flavoured herbs like rosemary,
thyme and oregano, and works equally well as a stand-alone feature,
as in the 'Roasted carrots' recipe below. *Salvia officinalis* is the sage
most often used for cooking, and while there are tricolour, golden
and purple sages available, they tend to have less flavour.
Sage forms a neat mound of aromatic grey-green foliage, and is as much
at home in the herb garden as it is in the cottage flower border. In areas
with harsh winters it can look a bit tatty through the cooler months, but in
most cases will bounce back again in late spring. Attractive spikes of white,
pink or pale blue flowers usually appear in late spring or early summer.

My favourite varieties

Three Colour Purple Carrot looks and tastes wonderful. In the garden it is fast growing and productive, and on the table it is positively intriguing. The skin is purple but the flesh is orange with a yellow core, so for greatest impact serve it with the skin on and sliced down the middle. The purple carrot originated in Afghanistan and still features strongly in the cuisine of this region. It was well known in Europe in the Middle Ages. In fact, it was the Dutch who crossed a purple carrot with a lemon-coloured one to yield the orange carrots we know today. The purple carrot does lose its pigment when cooked, so steam it lightly to retain some colour or serve it raw. This is a good variety for warmer climates.

Mini Round can be sown close together and, given its compact form, is the perfect variety for pots and heavy soils. I have had enormous success with Mini Round carrots in containers on the balcony. It's one of the few varieties suitable for transplanting as a seedling because it doesn't tend to fork with disturbance. Cook them whole and serve with melted butter.

Orange Chantenay is an heirloom variety originating in France, with large roots up to 15–20 centimetres long, which keep well through winter. Nowadays orange carrots are the most common types, but few can match the flavour of Orange Chantenay. Harvest the crop early for delicious baby carrots.

Yellow Austrian Lobbericher is well worth looking for, with its tasty yellow skin and flesh. Until recently yellow carrots were rare, yet despite being more readily available now they are still considered a novelty. The Austrian Lobbericher is commonly used in some countries as fodder for cattle or rabbits, but in others it is prized by gourmet cooks.

Belgian White is sometimes confused with parsnip as it produces pure white roots 20–25 centimetres long, with sweet white flesh. This is a popular variety in France and Belgium where it is used as forage for animals, but also in cooking. It is vigorous and productive, even in poor soils, and has a crisp, crunchy texture.

Carrot soup with orange and ginger

Serves 4

500 g carrots, chopped

1 onion, sliced

1 leek, sliced

2 tablespoons olive oil

1 litre chicken stock

juice of 2 oranges and zest of 1 orange

1 tablespoon sherry vinegar

1 cm cube ginger, grated

2 cloves garlic

1. Sweat the vegetables and ginger in oil until softened but not browned, then add stock, orange juice, garlic and vinegar. Simmer until carrot is tender.
2. Remove one cup of liquid and reserve. Puree all the other ingredients.
3. Adjust consistency with reserved liquid, finish with orange zest and serve.

Roasted carrots

Serves 4

500 g whole heirloom carrots, cleaned
1 tablespoon olive oil
8 fresh sage leaves
2 tablespoons honey

1. Preheat oven to 180°C.
Place carrots on a baking tray
and drizzle with olive oil.
2. Roast carrots whole for
approximately 45 minutes.
3. Remove from oven when soft and,
while still hot, quarter carrots and
toss with chopped sage and honey.
4. Return to oven for a further five
minutes, then serve.

Figs

There's something incredibly sensual about figs, with their lovely, delicate skin and mouth-watering flesh. It's no wonder that they are associated with delectable desserts. It's the edible fig (*Ficus carica*) that I'm writing about, not the huge rainforest species, which are hardly suitable for the average home garden. *Ficus carica* comes from the eastern Mediterranean. Its varieties are small- to medium-sized deciduous trees, which hover around 4–10 metres tall and bear heavy crops of juicy fruit.

Figs have old-fashioned charm and are often grown in gardens for their attractive shady canopy as well as their edible fruit. You'll always find them in old gardens and farmyards. My first memory of figs was the big old tree in my grandmother's garden, laden with a heavy crop that provided a feast for the family—and the birds!

Figs really enjoy a warm Mediterranean-type climate, but in cooler regions, you can take advantage of warm garden positions. In cool climates, figs perform well when espaliered against a sheltered south-facing wall. My grandma's fig certainly didn't suffer from her cool climate, sustaining good crops year after year in a warm sheltered position beside the house.

Figs are unusual in that their blossoms do not appear on the branches. Instead the tiny flowers are hidden inside the fig. Most varieties are self-fertile, meaning you need only one tree to produce a good crop. Under the right conditions, most figs will crop twice a year—in spring and autumn—but others, like White Adriatic, will produce just one crop. I don't remember Grandma's tree ever producing more than one.

Embryo figs (about the size of a pea) develop close to the tips of last season's growth and remain over winter. As spring progresses the young fruit begins to swell, and it's at this point that it is most susceptible to late-season frosts. The first crop of ripe figs is usually ready to pick in spring. During summer, the tree may also produce small fruitlets, which supply a second crop in late autumn. In cooler climates the first crop is usually the best, as the autumn crop rarely ripens before winter. Don't expect lots of fruit in the first year of planting; you'll get more from the second year onwards.

Health and nutrition

Figs have long been lauded in folklore for their cancer-fighting properties, and modern studies have

linked a compound found in figs to the shrinking of various tumours. Figs are also said to have anti-bacterial, anti-parasitic, anti-ulcer and laxative properties.

Rubbing the cut side of a fig against your teeth is an effective way to reduce decay-causing bacteria.

Growing

Figs prefer full sun, although they will cope with some morning shade, and they certainly don't need to be lavished with attention. In fact, a rich fertile soil and excess nitrogen can encourage leafy growth and no fruit. All they need is a light application of all-purpose flower and fruit fertiliser in spring. They are, however, fussy about drainage and may need to be planted on a mound. Figs prefer soils with a pH around 6–6.5, but will grow successfully in a broader range. They like a consistent supply of water during the growing season as fluctuating soil moisture when the fruit is developing can cause it to split.

Grandma's neglected and unpruned fig tree never ceased to produce a heavy crop of fruit. But in most gardens space dictates the need for pruning. At the very least, each year remove a few old, long branches that are largely unproductive to make way for new growth. Figs also benefit from a restricted root run which helps maintain a more manageable size for easy harvesting.

Figs are fabulous in small gardens and can be trained flat against a sunny courtyard wall. The wall provides both protection and additional warmth for the developing fruit. First, fix horizontal wires to the wall using metal eyes. Then use soft but strong twine to secure the branches to the wires. Your fig can be trained as an espalier (with horizontal arms) or as a fan shape.

Harvest

You'll know figs are ready to harvest when the fruit is hanging down and soft to touch. To pick, hold the stalk firmly and twist it away from the branch. Be aware that for some people the sap from the broken stem may be an irritant to the skin. Pick gently to avoid bruising the delicate skin. Fresh figs don't store particularly well and the fruit is best eaten straight from the tree or dried.

Kitchen

Figs are truly exquisite fruit, gathered for their sweet flesh and unique texture. They have equal appeal in both sweet and savoury dishes. I greedily consume figs straight from the tree, leaving nothing but the hard stalk end of the fruit. Others break them open and devour the succulent flesh. They are also a real treat baked whole and served with ice-cream, and you can turn excess fruit into delicious fig jam.

My favourite varieties

Brown Turkey is an old favourite, with large brown-skinned fruit late in the season. When you cut it open, the flesh is pink and has a rich, sweet flavour. It is lovely honey-roasted with mascarpone, pistachios and orange, dried, or made into tasty jam. This variety is adaptable and easy to grow. It is the most reliable fig in cooler climates.

White Genoa is another great one for cooler districts. The ripe fruit has pale green skin and amber-pink flesh, which is deliciously sweet. It is superb straight from the tree and one of the best for jam. It produces an early crop in spring, with a second crop in autumn.

Black Genoa is one of the best old cultivars available and a prolific fruiter from early spring. The pear-shaped fruit has green-purple skin and wonderfully textured light red flesh. It's a great eating variety, but not good for drying. It makes a lovely dish, wrapped in prosciutto and served with fetta.

White Adriatic is an attractive spreading fig tree, which bears large yellow-green skinned fruit with pink flesh and a strong flavour. It needs a long hot summer to ripen the fruit and produces just one crop. It is best peeled and devoured fresh, dried or made into jam.

Honey-roasted figs with mascarpone, pistachios and orange

Serves 4

8 figs
125 g mascarpone
½ handful unsalted, shelled pistachio nuts
2 tablespoons honey
1 orange, zest and juice

1. Preheat oven to 180°C. Place mascarpone, orange zest and juice, and half the honey in a bowl with half the pistachios, and mix.
2. Cut a lid across the top of each fig, leaving a hinge. Use a teaspoon to hollow out some of the soft flesh and spoon in the mascarpone mix.
3. Replace the lids and place figs close together in a baking dish so that they do not lose their shape during cooking. Drizzle with extra honey and nuts and bake for 15–20 minutes.
4. Serve at room temperature with good vanilla or orange-blossom ice-cream.

Figs with Persian fetta, wrapped in prosciutto

Serves 6

6 black figs

6 thin slices prosciutto

100 g Persian fetta

1 tablespoon fresh thyme, chopped

1 tablespoon lemon zest

Freshly ground black pepper, to taste

1. Cut figs in half vertically and lay cut side up.

2. Mix the fetta and some of its oil together with the thyme, black pepper and lemon zest, and spoon the mixture onto the fleshy part of the fig.

3. Depending on the size of the fig, wrap one or two pieces of prosciutto around each fig half. This can be served as a cold dish, or flash-grill the prosciutto until crisp and serve warmed.

Cucurbits: cucumbers, courgettes and pumpkins

Pumpkins, squash, cucumber and courgettes are all members of the Cucurbitaceae family, which grow from a prostrate vine. They come in a diverse range of shapes, sizes, colours and flavours. Being such prolific producers, there's always plenty to share around. Most varieties do take up room but make a good annual groundcover, and you can always maximise space by training them to grow up a trellis or over a shed or fence. There are also more compact-growing types, such as Bush Cucumber Spacemaster or Delicata Mini Sweet pumpkins, which perform well in large containers.

The courgette...

The courgette is in fact a baby marrow or summer squash. There are many kinds of courgette, including standard long and narrow varieties, like the heirloom Black Beauty, which can be harvested around two months after sowing, as well as the more unusual Crookneck varieties from America, which have thicker skin, a curved neck and bulbous ends. There is little difference in taste between them, but the curiously shaped Crooknecks are certainly a novelty and are often slightly sweeter than the standard types.

Health and nutrition

Cucumbers are a wonderful source of vitamins A and C, and the mineral potassium, which helps maintain regular fluid-balance and healthy nerve and muscle function. They have long been touted for their cosmetic properties, with records of their use dating back to early Egyptian times. The translation of an ancient papyrus, more than 2000 years old, revealed a recipe for a cucumber-based face mask that is said to have been the secret behind Cleopatra's beautiful complexion. A peeled and blended cucumber is also said to make an excellent lotion for the treatment of acne, and many swear by slices of fresh cucumber for relieving insect bites and for soothing tired and inflamed eyes.

Courgettes are more than 90 per cent water and are very low in kilojoules—approximately 63 kilojoules per 100 grams of fresh courgettes. They contain useful amounts of vitamin A, potassium and folic acid and small quantities of vitamin C and calcium.

Pumpkins are a good source of potassium and dietary fibre. They are also very high in beta-carotene, an antioxidant that stimulates the body's immune system and which has been linked to the

prevention of heart disease and various cancers. The beta-carotene is also converted to vitamin A in the body, helping to maintain healthy eyes, skin, hair, bones and teeth. Pumpkin seeds are an excellent source of zinc, which is necessary for hundreds of important enzymatic processes in the body.

Growing

All the cucurbits like plenty of sunshine and do best in rich, moisture-retentive, free-draining soil, with well-rotted manure and compost worked in. Cucumbers can be more sensitive to acidic soils than other cucurbits, so the addition of lime may be necessary in some instances. For those technically minded gardeners, a soil pH above 6.5 is what you're aiming for.

Cucurbits all benefit from mulching to help conserve moisture and suppress weeds. However, keep the mulch well away from the collar of plants, which are prone to rot. They also need plenty of water to support the large leaves and fleshy fruit. Once the fruit has set, a regular feed with a complete fertiliser will reward you with good results.

Cucurbits grow from prostrate vines and usually cover a lot of ground. The general rule is to allow about a square metre per plant for cucumber and courgette, and a little more for pumpkins. A lack of space should not deter you from growing cucurbits. Consider some of the more compact forms or make use of vertical space with climbing supports.

Each member of this family is prone to similar pests and diseases—the main problem being powdery mildew, a white talc-like substance which coats the leaves and is most prevalent under humid conditions. I always aim for prevention rather than treatment, achieved by planting in well-ventilated, sunny spots and by not watering from above. If treatment is necessary, many gardeners have had success with a milk-based spray rather than chemical solutions. Rotating your crops around the garden each season is also recommended to minimise soil-borne diseases.

All cucurbits are frost-sensitive and are grown as annuals. I direct-sow seeds in late spring, when

Courgettes can be brought to life with a little creativity in the kitchen

soil temperatures have warmed. Alternatively, you could give them a head start indoors, against a sunny window or in a greenhouse, and then transplant them into the garden when the risk of frost has passed. If required, protect young plants with cloches or frames in cool climates.

Members of the Cucurbitaceae family have separate male and female flowers on the one plant, and are pollinated by insects. Male flowers are needed to pollinate the female flowers and make the fruit swell. In some varieties, the ratio of male to female flowers can be affected by temperatures, stress and the number of daylight hours—factors which can impact on successful pollination.

You can manually aid pollination by picking a fully open male flower, stripping off the petals and brushing its stamens against the female's stigma, or by transferring pollen from the male to female flowers with a soft brush. To identify which is which, female flowers have an embryonic fruit (swelling) behind the flower petals, whereas the male flowers have just a thin stem.

PUMPKIN FOLKLORE

Native American folk remedy advocates the topical use of cold mashed pumpkin to relieve the pain and stimulate the healing of burns. Another folk remedy popular in parts of Europe and the former Soviet Union promotes the consumption of pumpkin seeds, which are high in certain amino acids believed to reduce the symptoms of prostate enlargement in men.

Harvest

I go out into the garden every day to harvest curcubits during the fruiting season as a staple for soups, stews and roasts. If you don't, they can quickly balloon to monstrous sizes with less culinary appeal.

Once cucumber plants are established, growth is rapid and you can usually expect a tasty crop about 11–12 weeks after sowing, and sometimes in as little as eight to nine weeks if conditions are favourable.

Courgettes grow prolifically and can seemingly double in size overnight. If the fruit is not picked regularly it will quickly develop into an oversized marrow, which I find offers little culinary inspiration apart from being stuffed and baked. For me, courgettes picked when they are roughly 10–15 cm in length offer the most flavour and versatility.

Most pumpkins are ready to pick around four months after sowing. The bright orange-skinned French variety, Rouge Vif d'Etampes, may be ready a month or so earlier. If they sound hollow when you give them a knock and the skin is nice and firm, then they're ready to harvest. The stems on ripe pumpkins also turn dry and brittle. Cut the stem a few centimetres above the pumpkin to avoid rotting. Some pumpkins last longer than others, but if you store them in a dry, airy spot many varieties will keep for months.

Kitchen

Cucumbers have a crisp texture and fresh flavour that is excellent in salads, sandwiches and cold soups. Their crunchy flesh is a great partner to yoghurt and garlic as a cooling accompaniment to spicy curry dishes or as a refreshing summer dip.

Many of the varieties of cucumber available are field cucumbers (slicing types for salads), although in recent years tiny fruited varieties such as the Lebanese Mini-Muncher have gained popularity and are also great for pickling or preserving.

Some people have an aversion to cucumbers because they tend to be bitter. Bitterness is influenced by a number of factors, but can be exacerbated by under-watering or leaving the fruit on the vine too long. The bitter taste is often concentrated in the skin and peeling them before eating is an option. This is rarely necessary in the 'burpless' varieties, where both the flavour and nutritional value is actually enhanced by leaving the skins intact. I usually discard the stalk end before eating as this is often quite bitter.

BURPLESS CUCUMBERS

For some people, eating cucumber may cause wind, but there are a range of hybrid and heirloom varieties that minimise discomfort. These are often described under the general term 'burpless cucumber', and may include varieties such as Burpless Telegraph, Lebanese Mini-Muncher and Armenian. There is also a current fashion for Apple Cucumbers, which are round with smooth white or yellow skin and excellent flavour.

Courgettes tend to have a delicate taste and texture, which can be brought to life with a little creativity in the kitchen. Courgettes are a favourite in my family, seasoned with stock, drizzled with olive oil and baked in the oven—simple but very tasty! They can also be used raw as crudités for dip, and combine well with other ingredients in soups, frittatas and vegetable stacks, or simply steamed and dressed with fresh herbs. The flowers are delicious dipped in batter and fried, stuffed with meat and cheese or added to risotto.

Pumpkins are a real favourite in kitchens. They are a delight to grow and there are many different varieties. In general, small-fruited pumpkins such as Delicata Mini Sweet and Red Kuri tend to be sweeter than larger fruiting types. Although technically a squash, 'Early Butternut' is a garden favourite, growing in a bush. The fruit has sweet, orange flesh that is wonderful baked and in soups. Of the large pumpkins, the Australian variety Queensland Blue is a great choice for its distinctive grey-blue skin and deep orange flesh, which keeps for ages and is ideal for baking because of its sweet taste. Then there are more boutique types, like the Japanese Hokkaido Squash, which has a unique chestnut flavour.

Oregano

Oregano is a popular herb in Italian and Greek-style cooking,
with wonderfully aromatic, slightly bitter tasting foliage.
Two or three sprigs are ideal in Tzatziki, the recipe for
which is included at the end of this chapter.
Oregano forms a neat bushy shrub to around 40 cm high, and has
the bonus of small pink flowers during summer, which are attractive
to friendly pollinators like bees and butterflies. Trim it back after
flowering to encourage bushy plants. There is also a more
compact golden-leafed variety, which makes a great
decorative border around the herb or flower garden.

My favourite varieties

Armenian Cucumbers can grow to 60–90 centimetres in length and are heavily ribbed. The young cucumbers are lime green, turning paler with age. When the fruit changes to a light mustard colour it is ripe to pick and has a strong odour. The young skin is burpless and thin, so the fruit is often used without peeling. It is mostly used for pickling, or harvested young and eaten fresh.

Lebanese Mini-Muncher Cucumber is one of the best salad varieties available. As the name suggests, the cucumbers are small, crunchy and sweet, with smooth skin that isn't bitter. They are perfect for slicing straight into salads and are tailor-made for pickling.

Bohemian Pumpkin is a rare and beautiful heirloom variety with mottled pink and blue-green skin, and sweet orange flesh. It produces medium-sized pumpkins up to 9.2 kilograms in weight. If it's tasty pumpkin soup you're after, you can't beat the Bohemian.

World's Largest Pumpkin is an aptly named heirloom variety that produced the world's largest pumpkin, weighing a whopping 402 kilograms, and it is not unusual to harvest pumpkins up to 230 kilograms. It's a favourite with the kids and ideal for gardening competitions, but not great eating.

Black Beauty Courgette is a great variety for most gardens. It's prolific and easy to grow. The plant is relatively compact and the fruit isn't too big. It produces an abundance of glossy, black-green fruit with creamy white flesh throughout the summer. The fruit is best eaten when it is roughly 15–20 centimetres long, around 50–60 days after planting. It is best steamed and garnished with fresh herbs, or dressed in oil, oven-roasted and served in a vegetable stack.

Crookneck Early Summer Courgette is a prolific old variety of summer squash with a distinctly 'crooked' neck. It's a bush type that produces brilliant yellow fruit with a slightly warted skin and smooth, creamy white flesh. Fruits are best picked when they are around 12–15 centimetres long, when the flesh is sweetest, although fruits left on the vine too long can still be used for decoration.

Grilled courgette

Serves 2

300 g courgette
3 tablespoons olive oil
Salt and pepper, to taste
Parmesan cheese, grated, to garnish

1. Slice the courgettes lengthwise into long strips that are roughly 5 mm thick.
2. Grill both sides of each slice in a hot skillet with a little olive oil until lightly coloured.
3. Arrange the grilled courgettes on a plate, season with salt and pepper, and serve garnished with grated parmesan.

Tzatziki

Serves 2

500 g Greek-style yoghurt, drained for one hour in a muslin-lined sieve or colander
1 Lebanese cucumber, peeled and grated
1 garlic clove, crushed
1 lemon, zest and juice
3 sprigs of oregano, chopped
Salt and pepper, to taste

1. Combine all ingredients and season to taste.
2. Chill until ready to serve.

Pumpkin gnocchi
Serves 2

750 g roasted pumpkin, mashed

100 g semolina

50 g parmesan cheese, grated

5 eggs, whisked

1 brown onion, finely chopped

2 cloves garlic, finely chopped

100 g butter

Salt and pepper, to taste

1. Sauté the onions and garlic in butter until soft but not browned.
2. Combine all the ingredients and place into a greased shallow baking tray. Spread mixture so it is evenly distributed and sprinkle with extra parmesan cheese.
3. Bake in a moderate oven until golden (approximately 20 minutes).
4. Turn out of the tray and cut the gnocchi into the desired shape for serving with a tomato-based pasta sauce.

Brassicas:
broccoli,
cauliflower
and cabbage

The brassicas are a group of vegetables that all come from the same wild ancestor, *Brassica oleracea*. Cabbage, cauliflower, broccoli and brussels sprout are some of the most common and often find a place in my garden, but the genus also includes varieties like kale, mustard and many leafy Asian greens.

There are varieties for every season, but it's in winter, when there are less things to grow in the vegetable garden (especially in cooler climates), that they really come into their own, particularly for hearty soups, pastas and stews. Winter-grown crops also tend to be less prone to attack by cabbage white butterfly, which can be a real pest in summer.

It's certainly worth growing one or two varieties for their culinary value alone, but don't underestimate the decorative role they can also play in the garden. Whether it be the steely blue January King cabbages, the rich purple leaves of Red Drum Head Cabbage or Tuscan Black Kale, whose leaf colour falls somewhere between purple-blue and midnight, these varieties add presence and colour to the garden. They can be planted in bold groups in your vegetable plot or mingled with other vegetables and flowers.

The familiar cauliflower has white heads, but we are also experiencing a resurgence of heirloom varieties with green, pink, purple or orange heads that are wonderfully flavoured. Purple Cape is a real show-stopper, with large dusky-purple heads. Look out for more of these varieties as they become available for something different in the garden and the kitchen.

CABBAGE

Cabbages are sometimes categorised by their appearance. Some have crinkled or deeply wrinkled leaves, like Savoy. Others are described as drum heads, with round compact heads and smooth leaves. Then there are the pointed cabbages with conical heads. There are also novelty types with blue leaves and red heads, whose colour intensifies with the cold and which are wonderfully ornamental in the kitchen garden.

Health and nutrition

All brassicas are known as cruciferous, a group of vegetables that have long been touted for their health-promoting benefits. They were revered in ancient Rome as a cancer cure, and in the Middle Ages were referred to as 'the drug of the poor'. They contain many phytochemicals, including indoles and

dithioliones, which studies have linked to protection against stomach, colon, breast and ovarian cancer, and glucosinolates, which are believed to enhance the removal of toxic substances from the body. Brassicas also contain sulphur compounds, which are considered to have antibiotic and antiviral properties.

By weight, fresh broccoli that has been lightly boiled and drained contains close to 20 per cent more vitamin C than oranges and about the same amount of calcium as milk. It is high in beta-carotene and a good source of iron, which supports the immune system in the production of white blood cells and antibodies, and helps to carry oxygen around the body.

As well as vitamin C and beta-carotene, cauliflower and cabbage are good sources of vitamin B3, which promotes healthy skin and regulates blood-sugar levels. Cabbage also contains vitamin K, which is essential for normal blood clotting, and the red varieties are believed to have antiseptic properties that help fight infection. Cabbage is also thought to contain compounds that help to heal gastric ulcers.

Some of the benefits of these vegetables are believed to be lost in cooking, so it's good to include some raw produce in the diet and favour light cooking techniques such as steaming and stir-frying.

Growing

All brassicas share a preference for an open position and rich well-drained soil, so the ground should be prepared by adding compost and rotted manure. They are a good leafy crop to follow legumes, which produce their own soil nitrogen. Brassicas are sensitive to acidity—particularly cauliflowers, which need a pH above 6.5 to grow best—so dig in a couple of handfuls of lime when preparing the ground. Effective drainage is important to prevent fungal disease, so grow them in raised beds or mounds if needed.

If you're growing brassicas from seed, it is best to sow them into punnets and transplant them into the garden as young seedlings, or you can buy them as ready-grown seedlings from your nursery. Give them regular applications of organic fertiliser and a consistent supply of water to encourage full-sized heads and, in the case of cabbages, to prevent splitting.

Brassicas are all predisposed to similar pests and diseases which can stay in the soil after the plants are removed, so it's a good idea to rotate the crop each year with onions, legumes and root crops. It's worth noting that commercially grown brassicas are often one of the most heavily sprayed crops in

order to prevent damage by the cabbage white butterfly—so it's definitely worth growing your own.

If you are thinking about growing brassicas in small spaces, try some of the more compact types such as mini cauliflower or cabbage, which can be grown closer together or in containers on a patio or balcony. If you're growing them in pots, a good-quality potting mix, consistent watering and regular liquid feeding will promote the best results.

Broccoli seedlings are available from early spring for summer cropping, but with a preference for a winter crop I sow my broccoli seeds in mid-summer or plant seedlings in autumn for harvesting during winter and early spring.

Some cabbage varieties are more susceptible to splitting in the summer heat, so in frost-free areas it may be advisable to hold off planting until late summer or autumn for harvesting in winter and early spring. Being slower to develop in winter, they lend themselves to intercropping with faster growing greens such as spinach and silverbeet, providing a continuous supply of leafy produce. However, in frosty areas a summer crop may be the way to go, and I would suggest the lime green-headed Golden Acre or the heirloom Red Drum Head, which are more heat-tolerant and can be planted out in spring to ripen at the same time as your beans and first tomatoes.

CAULIFLOWER DISCOLOURATION

You might notice a yellow discolouration in some cauliflower heads,
particularly those grown at home. This is caused by exposure to intense
sunlight, but is less likely in cauliflower varieties that are self-blanching
(meaning that the leaves grow around the developing head to protect it).
In the more open varieties you could try tying some of the bigger leaves
together above the head to shade them and preserve the pure white
curds. This is not such a problem if seedlings are planted in autumn
because they mature in mid-spring when there is less heat and sunlight.

Harvest

Modern broccolis have been developed to produce squatter growth and large compact central heads, and therefore don't tend to have side shoots. Original Italian heirloom varieties like Calabrese are

Broccoli is one of the
few green vegetables
that kids like
to eat and some
purple varieties are
a culinary delight

useful as sprouting broccoli. After the central head has been cut, these varieties produce side shoots which can be harvested for a number of months. Cut the central head of sprouting broccoli early in the season to encourage delicious side shoots, and remember to harvest the head before the flowers start to burst or you'll prevent side heads from forming.

Green Sprouting Broccoli is one of the best sprouting varieties, with tender blue-green heads that can be repeat-picked for ages. There are also purple sprouting varieties that are as pleasing in the garden as they are on the plate. Another type, Romanesco Broccoli, has a delicate flavour particularly popular in Europe. It matures later in the season and produces a spiral of compact lime-green heads. But once you've cut the head, don't expect any side shoots.

Cauliflower seedlings planted in spring and early summer can be harvested in autumn and early winter. For an early summer crop, sow seeds in autumn in a greenhouse or under glass. Harvest the curds of cauliflower when they are compact and solid.

To pick cabbage heads, cut the stem a few centimetres above the ground, leaving a small stump and the outer leaves. There's a good chance it will re-sprout and produce another crop of baby cabbage.

Kitchen

In my experience, broccoli is one of the few green vegetables that kids like to eat. As a child my mother used to call broccoli 'trees', which made it all the more appealing. The 'tree canopy'—the best part to eat—is actually the head of unopened flower buds which, if left unpicked, develop into a sea of yellow.

Like broccoli, it is the unopened flower head on cauliflower that we eat. Cauliflower may be rather bland to taste but it absorbs strong flavours well and goes with almost any kind of food. Depending on what time of year you're harvesting your crop, cauliflower can make a wonderful addition to soups, casseroles and curry dishes in winter, and is great tossed raw in salads or chopped and served with dip in the summer months.

Cabbages harvested in winter and early spring provide a bountiful supply for adding to soups, or for use as a side dish cooked gently with sautéed onions or butter and caraway seeds. Summer crops provide raw leaves perfect for salads and coleslaw. Ornamental cabbages and kales are valued in the kitchen for their decorative leaf colouring and serrated, wavy or frilly leaves. Try using some of the novelty types with blue leaves and red heads to provide a distinctive colour contrast in coleslaw or

green salads. They are also delicious braised with orange zest, spices and red wine vinegar, as described in the recipe for 'Braised purple cabbage' on page 146.

CHERVIL

Chervil is a staple ingredient in classic French cooking. It joins chives, tarragon and parsley as a common ingredient in the aromatic seasoning blend called *fines herbes*, and is often used to flavour eggs, fish, chicken and light sauces. Try it out with brassicas, too, using the recipes for 'Broccolini with chervil and anchovy vinaigrette' and 'Cauliflower fritters' at the end of this chapter.

Chervil has bright green foliage that resembles carrot tops and tastes a little like liquorice. Chervil prefers a cool, moist, shaded location and will bolt to seed in extremes of heat or cold. As the leaves mature they take on hints of bronze and purple and lose their intensity of flavour, so the young tender leaves make the best picking. Sow seed in succession every few weeks during spring and summer for a longer harvest of fresh young leaves. In milder areas seed can be sown in autumn. Sow the seed where plants are to grow, because it doesn't transplant well.

My favourite varieties

Romanesco Broccoli is a variety widely grown and valued in Italy where it was first described in the 16th century. It is commonly called Broccolo Romanesco, or Romanesco Broccoli, although it is sometimes known as Cavolo Romanesco (Romanesco Cabbage). It forms a single lime green spiralling head 20–30 centimetres across, and has a fine taste and texture that can be enjoyed steamed, stir-fried or smothered in white sauce. Romanesco Broccoli doesn't produce many side shoots, so once the main head has been cut plants can be dug up and composted.

Green Sprouting Broccoli produces sweet blue-green heads which can be harvested for months. Harvest some of the heads as soon as they form to encourage more side shoots. It has four times the

yield of hybrid single-headed types. This is the star ingredient in our 'Broccolini with chervil and anchovy vinaigrette'. There are also purple sprouting varieties that are a culinary delight.

Mini Cauliflower is ideal for growing in pots on the balcony or in tight garden spaces. Plant it 30 centimetres apart for delicious bite-sized heads just 10 centimetres in diameter. It's perfect for tasty cauliflower fritters and great for kids.

Red Drum Head Cabbage is an incredibly decorative variety with steely blue outside leaves concealing a deep purple-red centre. I have often planted groups of Red Drum Head cabbages among coloured silverbeet and flowers in the cottage garden to fill the space until spring. It's divine braised or finely shredded and used in coleslaw.

Tuscan Kale is proof that cabbage doesn't have to be boring. Tuscan Kale, or Cavolo Nero as it is also known, is an Italian kale with slate-grey foliage and crinkled leaves, making it striking in the garden and the kitchen. It has a strong 'cabbagey' flavour, with an almost sweet aftertaste, and can be boiled without losing its texture or colour. Tuscan Kale is lovely braised with onion and garlic, is perfect with pork, or can be used to make decorative cabbage rolls. It's particularly good in thick, rich soups like classic Tuscan soup.

Broccolini with anchovy vinaigrette

Serves 4

In a mortar and pestle, mince:

  2 cloves garlic

  2 anchovy fillets

  1 teaspoon salt

  1 dessertspoon chopped chervil

2 bunches broccolini

2 tablespoons vinaigrette (see page 189)

1. In a stainless steel bowl add $\frac{1}{2}$ teaspoon of the anchovy mixture to two tablespoons of vinaigrette and stir to combine.

2. Blanch the broccolini in a little salted water until just tender, drain, and while hot coat the broccolini with dressing and serve.

Braised purple cabbage

Serves 4

$\frac{1}{2}$ purple cabbage, shredded

100 ml red wine vinegar

100 g brown sugar

2 star anise

1 cinnamon stick

1 naval orange, juice and zest

1 teaspoon caraway seeds

100 g raisins

1. Place all the ingredients except the cabbage into a stainless steel pot and bring to the boil.

2. Add the cabbage and braise slowly on low heat for 20 minutes or until tender. Remove cinnamon and star anise and serve.

Cauliflower fritters

Serves 4

1 mini cauliflower cut into small florets
2 large eggs
2 tablespoons plain flour
2 tablespoons breadcrumbs
1 tablespoon chervil, chopped
1 tablespoon flat parsley, chopped
1 tablespoon chives
Salt and freshly ground black pepper, to taste
1 cup olive oil for frying

1. Steam florets until soft, drain and pat dry,
and then mash half the florets and reserve the
remaining quantity.
2. Whisk the eggs, then add flour, breadcrumbs,
chervil, parsley and chives together with a pinch
of salt and freshly ground black pepper to taste.
Add a little milk if the mixture is too dry,
and fold in all the cauliflower—both mashed
and florets.
3. Heat olive oil and gently fry one heaped
tablespoon of the cauliflower mixture over
medium heat until lightly golden. Drain on
kitchen paper and serve as is, or with smoked
salmon, crème fraîche and extra chervil.

Tagliatelle with broccoli, red pepper flakes and garlic

Serves 4

Make a quantity of basic pasta dough or use good dried semolina pasta. Cook the pasta until just soft in plenty of salted water. Drain and keep warm.

1 small head of young broccoli
1 dessertspoon dried red pepper flakes
2 tablespoons of good olive oil
2–3 cloves of garlic, finely chopped
Salt and freshly ground pepper
Extra olive oil or parmesan cheese

1. Blanch the broccoli in boiling water for two minutes, then rinse in cold water and drain.
2. Cut into small florets and discard the stalks.
3. In a medium-sized frypan gently heat the olive oil and add the garlic, red pepper flakes and florets. Stir to warm through, but do not allow the garlic to brown.
4. Add the tagliatelle and keep tossing until warmed through.
5. Add a little extra olive oil or freshly grated parmesan cheese to serve.

Twice-cooked cauliflower soufflé

Serves 6

100 g cauliflower

50 g butter

90 g plain flour

Pinch of salt, pepper and nutmeg

250 ml milk

3 egg yolks

3 egg whites, beaten

100 g grated cheese

375 ml pouring cream

Extra cheese

1. Steam cauliflower for 5 minutes or until tender. Place the cauliflower and 1 tablespoon of the cooking water in a blender and puree. Set aside.

2. Preheat the oven to 180°C.

3. Melt the butter in a saucepan over low heat, add the flour, nutmeg, salt and pepper and stir for approximately one minute. Remove saucepan from heat and stir in the milk, then place back over the heat and continue to stir until the mixture thickens to the consistency of a firm white sauce. Allow the mixture to cool.

4. Mix in the egg yolks, cheese and cauliflower puree, and once the ingredients are well combined fold in the beaten egg whites.

5. Grease 6 small ramekins with butter and fill to two thirds with mixture. Place the ramekins in a deep oven tray and pour warm water into the tray to halfway up the side of the ramekins. Bake in the oven for approximately 25 minutes, then remove and allow to cool. (Do not turn off the oven.)

6. Turn the soufflés out from the ramekins and place on a slightly cream-moistened gratin dish. Pour cream over the soufflés and top with some extra cheese. Bake in the oven till they rise again and turn golden.

Citrus

For me, there's nothing like the sweet scent of citrus blossom wafting in the air and the taste of ripe fruit fresh from your own citrus tree. These versatile plants have so much going for them—lush, glossy green leaves, pretty white blossoms and, in the right spot, they will produce a bountiful supply of fruit.

Many people mistakenly believe that in cool climates you need a sophisticated 'orangery' or conservatory to grow citrus successfully. In fact, all you need is a warm, sheltered, frost-free spot. There are also several varieties of citrus, such as the Seville orange and cumquat, which are adaptable to cooler regions.

Citrus trees have been grown in Asian and Mediterranean gardens for centuries for their heavily scented blossoms and luxuriant beauty. And they haven't lost their appeal—in fact, they're perfect for modern gardens. They can be clipped, espaliered, trained into vase shapes, grown in giant terracotta pots or displayed in formal rows to create a Mediterranean effect.

Growing citrus in containers is not only decorative but practical. Potted citrus trees can be moved under cover in winter, into a greenhouse or indoors. While citrus can be grown indoors year-round, this can hamper their ability to bear fruit. A sunny, sheltered spot during the frost-free months will be greatly appreciated—and rewarding.

Health and nutrition

Citrus has long being renowned for its vitamin C content, and has traditionally been used to relieve sore throats and reduce the symptoms associated with cold and flu. The benefits of vitamin C go well beyond its immune-boosting capacity. It is also essential for the formation of collagen, a core component in much of the connective tissue in the body. Collagen is necessary for strong ligaments, tendons and skin, and is critical in wound-healing and tissue-repair. Vitamin C also helps the absorption of iron, and is a powerful antioxidant that is believed to prevent cell damage and inhibit the development of various disease states, including cardiovascular disease, certain cancers and cataracts in the eyes.

Citrus fruits are also a source of dietary fibre, beta-carotene and folic acid, and are said to contain over 100 different phytochemicals in their flesh and rind, which not only multiply the antioxidant effects, but are also believed to have anti-inflammatory, anti-viral and anti-allergic properties.

Growing

Most citrus originate in South-East Asia and India, and are frost-tender. However, many species will survive short periods of 0°C. The easiest citrus trees to grow in cooler climates are lemons, particularly varieties that have been grafted onto an appropriate rootstock. (Ask your nursery when buying your tree.) Also good for frosty zones are Meyer lemons, Wheeny grapefruit, Seville oranges, sweet oranges and cumquats.

In frost-free areas you can try all types of citrus, bearing in mind that some limes prefer a subtropical climate. This is particularly the case with the kaffir lime, whose wonderfully fragrant leaves are delicious in Thai dishes. The giant pomelo, a Malaysian native, also prefers warm climates. This grapefruit-like citrus has thick, soft rind and pale pink flesh.

Citrus trees like full sun. They will grow in some shade, but produce lots of leafy growth and less fruit if there's not enough light. They need very well-drained soil. A slightly acidic, loamy soil is ideal. Before planting, dig in a good amount of well-rotted organic matter. In poorly drained conditions, grow citrus in large pots or raised beds.

Citrus trees are shallow-rooted, so to keep them in tip-top condition mulch and give them a reasonably consistent supply of water, particularly when they're young or when fruit is developing. If not, maturing fruit may split. Apply mulch a hand's span clear of the trunk to avoid stem-rot diseases.

Citrus need to be fertilised regularly to sustain growth and good fruiting. Apply a complete citrus food or organic fertiliser each month from the first new growth in spring through to summer. Feeding after summer forces citrus into late growth in autumn, which attracts citrus leaf miner that may deform the leaves. Water the tree well before and after feeding. Also add a layer of compost enriched with well-rotted manure in spring—this keeps uniform moisture around the root zone and helps prevent problems such as fruit splitting or roots drying out.

When citrus trees are grown in cold climates, it's not uncommon for leaves to yellow in winter. A complete fertiliser at the first sign of growth in spring remedies this.

It's best to remove developing fruit on a young tree for one or two years so it can put its energy into growth and development. This results in a healthier plant with a good framework for future fruiting. Even with mature plants, it's worth thinning heavy crops so the tree doesn't exhaust itself.

Always use good-quality potting mix for citrus in containers. If required, repot citrus in spring.

Older, established trees that can't be repotted can have their potting mix refreshed instead. Simply remove the top 5–10 centimetres of the old potting mix—taking care not to damage the roots—and replace with fresh mix.

Remember, the height of your citrus tree will depend on the type of rootstock it's on and your own growing conditions. They can all be pruned to the desired shape and height. Cut off dead and diseased wood and crossing branches once the danger of frost has passed. They are easily shaped—you can even use hedge clippers. This forces the tree into forming multiple shoots, which form masses of flowers and fruit on their tips.

SPACE-SAVER TIP

If you're pressed for space or have a courtyard, follow the example of
Mediterranean gardeners and grow citrus trees in terracotta pots filled
with good-quality potting mix. Varieties that have been grafted onto dwarf
rootstocks are well suited to this, and they often flower and fruit earlier.
Petite cumquats make wonderful potted plants, as do calamondins.
Also suitable are Meyer lemons and Tahitian limes because
they don't grow too large. Of course, all citrus can be grown
in pots because the container acts as a dwarfing mechanism.

Harvest

Some citrus, such as oranges, cumquats, grapefruits, mandarins and Tahitian limes, flower once a year and, with the help of bees, blossoms are followed by a good crop of fruit. In warm conditions, prolific lemons like Meyer and Lisbon hardly go a week without fruit or blossom.

Citrus fruits can take six to eight months to ripen, depending on the climate. The cooler the temperature, the longer it takes. Lack of sufficient sunshine can also result in citrus fruits remaining green. Oranges, in particular, ripen over a long season, depending on the variety.

Kitchen

Citrus adds zest to many dishes. The juice, flesh or rind can be used in sauces, dressings, desserts, cakes, drinks and preserves. A gin and tonic isn't complete without a wedge of fresh lime or lemon, orange rind is essential for good marmalade and the leaves of kaffir limes are a core ingredient in Thai cooking. Check out the suggested kitchen uses for my favoured citrus varieties.

My favourite varieties

Seville or *Sour Orange* is an evergreen tree that grows up to 9 metres tall, but is also available on a dwarf rootstock or can be kept smaller through pruning. It produces a heavy crop of big pale-orange, squat-shaped fruit. The fruit is sour and filled with seeds so it's not great eating, but it's ideal for making marmalade and jelly. It is one of the more cold-hardy varieties.

Chinotto is a compact shrub to 2 metres that's perfect in pots. It has dark green leaves and produces bitter orange golf ball-sized fruit. The weight of the fruit gives the tree a lovely weeping habit. A good marmalade fruit, it's also used in Italian soft drinks.

Kaffir Lime is an evergreen shrub that only reaches 3 metres in height, making it ideal for tubs. Pick the leaves regularly to keep it compact. The leaves and small knobbly fruit are used to flavour Asian dishes. Beware, the branches can be quite thorny. It's best suited to warmer climates, but will grow in cooler areas in pots, in a warm sheltered position.

Tangelo is the juiciest of all citrus! This cross between a mandarin and a grapefruit is slightly tart, making it ideal for juicing or adding to desserts. An evergreen tree, it can reach 9 metres, but can be kept under 3 metres by pruning.

Lane's Late Navel is like a Washington navel, having large, seedless good-quality fruit, but it crops later. The sweet fruit is great eaten fresh or juiced. It can grow up to 6 metres tall, but it is easily pruned. It's quite a frost-hardy orange, suitable to colder climes.

Joppa is an old variety of orange that should be more widely grown. An evergreen tree that can reach 6 metres, it fruits heavily and reliably. This tree produces medium to large fruit with consistently good flavour—perfect for juicing and eating fresh.

Blood Oranges are increasingly favoured for the fruit's amazing red flesh and juice. In general, cooler conditions produce better colour.

Lemonade has fruit that look like lemons but are sweeter and are best eaten fresh or used for lemonade. This frost-tolerant tree produces big crops and responds well to additional fertiliser.

Limes are excellent in pots due to their naturally small size. Most prefer warm climates, though the Tahitian lime is suitable for cooler conditions.

Cumquats originate in China and are the most cold-hardy of citrus, coping with temperatures of –5°C for short periods. Perfect for pots, they produce small yellow fruits that are usually eaten unpeeled.

Unusual varieties

Calamondin is a hybrid between a mandarin and a cumquat. Its orange fruit can be dried or used in jams. The 2.5 metre-tall tree makes a lovely potted shrub.

Citron is also called *Buddha's Hand* and *Fingered Citron* because its golden fruit splits into finger-like segments. As the fruit doesn't have flesh, this tree, which grows to 6 metres, is largely ornamental. But the fruit has a nice sweet scent and can be put in a bowl to perfume a room.

Pomelo bears fruit that grows up to 30 centimetres wide with thick, green-yellow skin and a sweet, tangy flavour like grapefruit. This tree grows to about 6 metres tall.

Mini meringues with lemon curd

Meringues

200 ml egg whites

250 g caster sugar

20 g corn flour

200 g caster sugar

10 ml white vinegar

1. Whisk egg whites to form stiff peaks while adding 250 g sugar, a third at a time.
2. Sieve together the cornflour and 200 g sugar, fold into the meringue mixture and then fold in the white vinegar.
3. Spoon 1 tablespoon amounts of meringue mixture onto a baking tray lined with baking paper. You should end up with about 18.
4. Bake in a preheated oven at 165 °C for 20 minutes. Remove and leave to cool.

Lemon curd

5 egg yolks

100 g caster sugar

110 ml lemon juice

125 g unsalted butter

1. Whisk the egg yolks and sugar in a bowl until fluffy, then add the lemon juice.
2. Place the bowl over a saucepan with water and slowly heat, stirring until thickened.
3. Add the butter gradually, stirring until combined. Remove from heat and cool over a bowl of ice.
4. Join two mini meringues together with the lemon curd filling and serve with cream.

Lemon tart

Serves 10

Pastry

500 g plain flour

100 g caster sugar

Pinch of salt

250 g unsalted butter, chopped

2 eggs, beaten

1 tablespoon water

Filling

9 eggs, lightly beaten

400 g caster sugar

Juice of 5 lemons

Finely grated zest of 2 lemons

250 ml double cream

1. To make the pastry, sift the flour, sugar and salt into a large bowl and rub in the butter until the mixture resembles breadcrumbs. Make a well in the centre and pour in the eggs and water. Use a flat bladed knife to mix together until combined then gather the dough into a ball. Flatten out to a thick disc, wrap in plastic wrap and refrigerate for 30 minutes.

2. Preheat the oven to 180°C. Roll out the pastry and use to line a 30 cm loose-bottomed flan tin. Trim the edges, and cover with a sheet of non-stick baking paper. Fill with dried beans or rice, place onto a baking tray, and bake for 15 minutes. Reduce the oven to 175°C.

3. Combine the filling ingredients and carefully pour into the pastry case. Return to the oven and cook for about 25 minutes, until the custard is set. Leave in the tin for 15 minutes before removing the flan ring.

Lemon brulee

Serves 10

7 whole eggs
4 egg yolks
300 ml lemon juice
600 ml pure cream
1 cup caster sugar
$\frac{1}{2}$ cup caster sugar

1. Preheat the oven to 150°C. Combine the eggs, yolks and sugar in a large bowl and whisk until smooth. Add the lemon juice and cream and stir to combine.
2. Pour the mixture into 10 x 110 ml capacity ramekins. Place the ramekins into a large baking dish. Pour enough water into the baking dish to come halfway up the sides of the ramekins.
3. Place the baking dish into the oven and bake for 50–60 minutes, until the custard is just set. Remove from the oven and let the ramekins cool in the baking dish.
4. Place $\frac{1}{2}$ cup caster sugar into a small frying pan and melt the sugar over medium heat. Swirl the sugar in the pan until it is golden brown but not burnt. Remove from heat immediately and pour a little on top of each of the custards.

Orange blossom oil

Makes 2 cups

finely grated zest of 1 orange
50 ml orange blossom water
500 ml cold pressed olive oil

1. Place all the ingredients into a glass or stainless steel jug.
2. Allow to steep overnight, then strain into a bottle and seal.
3. Use as dressing for Five-Colour Silverbeet (see page 188).

Potatoes

In the garden, potatoes can take up a lot of space for a long period, and being so cheap to buy, why would you bother growing them? Well, for a start, commercial potatoes are often grown using big doses of chemicals—something which definitely doesn't appeal to me. By growing your own you also get to experience the superior flavour of garden-harvested spuds and you can grow unique varieties that you will never find in shops.

The potatoes I like to grow are the 'gourmet' type—those varieties, often with yellow flesh, that are sought after by top chefs and restaurants. Forget the familiar white-fleshed, pale-skinned 'fast-food chip-making' spud. There is a wide choice of potatoes to grow, each with something different to offer in terms of flavour, texture and appearance, cooking quality and resistance to pests and disease.

Most of the potatoes that we grow can be traced back to the first potato varieties introduced to Europe from South America, their native homeland, where they have been cultivated for thousands of years.

As a member of the Solanaceae family, the potato is closely related to tomatoes, capsicums, chillies and eggplant. It is a perennial plant with hairy stems, large dark green leaves and clusters of pretty white, mauve or pink flowers. The leaves and flowers of potatoes are poisonous. So are any tubers which have turned green as a result of exposure to light.

Potatoes are often categorised by the number of days they take to mature, which can be anywhere from 75 to 150 days, depending on the variety. This is an important consideration when choosing your varieties, particularly given they may occupy considerable space in the garden for a long period. Early types are generally lower yielding and so take up less space, and tend to make good salad potatoes. Slower maturing varieties usually grow larger and have higher yields.

Health and nutrition

Not only do they taste good, but potatoes are a wonderful source of carbohydrate, making them an excellent fuel food. They also contain vitamin C, and the B vitamins thiamine (B1), niacin (B3) and pyridoxine (B6). B vitamins are water soluble, meaning they are not stored by the body and should therefore be consumed daily. They are necessary for carbohydrate metabolism, the maintenance of healthy nervous and digestive systems, muscle functioning and coordination, and the formation of red blood cells. Potatoes also provide moderate amounts of iron, phosphorous and potassium.

Growing

I make it a rule to always use fresh certified seed potatoes. (Seed potatoes saved from last season or bought from the fruit shop may look healthy, but using them can lead to a build-up of viruses and disease.) They're also high-yielding and easy to grow. Seed potatoes aren't actually 'seed', but rather tubers. In fact they look just like small potatoes.

In cooler regions, like where I live, it's best to wait until late winter or early spring before planting to avoid young shoots being damaged by frost. I sow my first seed potatoes outdoors in early spring, in a well-drained, sunny spot in rich soil that has been prepared first with rotted manure and compost. In just a few short weeks the first shoots are poking their way through the soil and by early summer you should be enjoying a bountiful harvest. Late, or maincrop, varieties can be planted in mid to late spring for autumn harvest.

If space can be found, set the rows 60 centimetres to 1 metre apart, dig good deep holes, planting tubers roughly 10–15 centimetres deep and 35–40 centimetres apart with the potato eye pointing upwards. Large seed potatoes can be cut into pieces first, but should be left to dry out before planting to prevent them rotting in the ground. There should be at least one or two 'eyes' or buds on each cut piece.

Once the potatoes are growing, rake some soil up around the shoots to form a mound. This prevents light from reaching the tubers and turning them green. It also helps to mulch with a thick layer of straw, which has the added benefit of conserving moisture.

When growth is at its peak keep the water up, particularly during flowering and immediately after when the tubers are growing.

SMALL AREAS

Potatoes do take up a reasonable amount of space, but it's a small price to pay for a tasty, bountiful crop. In small gardens, it's worth finding a spot to grow at least a few potatoes. If space is limited, then plant just one or two mounds. Otherwise, I have certainly had success with fast-maturing early varieties such as Nicola growing in deep pots, and a friend of mine grows them in layers in a cylindrical tower made from a length of bamboo fencing about a metre high. This makes the most of vertical space.

Harvest

When the stems and foliage have yellowed and died off, it's time to harvest your potatoes. Start by harvesting well outside each plant, that way you can dig and eat your potatoes as you need them. Each tuber produces roughly another ten potatoes, and I have found that just three or four seed potatoes will give a small family plenty to eat.

'New' potatoes can be lifted from the time the flowers open fully. New potatoes are immature, so they're smaller and firmer, and need only be washed and boiled until just tender. They don't store well so try to eat them quickly or dig and use them as you need to. You might even like to plant early varieties into the garden mid-season, so you can harvest your new baby potatoes later.

STORAGE

Potatoes can last for months if they are stored in a cool, dark, well-ventilated place. When potatoes are exposed to light they start to turn green, in which case they shouldn't be eaten as they can be poisonous. Avoid any plastic packaging, because it causes potatoes to sweat.

Kitchen

Potatoes combine well with a variety of herbs and flavourings. By themselves they aren't fattening; it's the rich additions like butter and cream that make them sinful, but also delicious to eat!

The texture of a potato often reveals how it is best cooked. The waxy, moister varieties such as Kipfler tend to remain intact after cooking so are best for boiling and steaming—these are the ones for potato salad. Incidentally, it is best to boil potatoes with their skin on to help maintain their flavour and vitamin content. It's also less trouble to leave skins on. The oddly shaped varieties are also easier to peel with your fingers after boiling. On the other hand, dryer types such as Desiree become light and fluffy after cooking, and are ideal for baking, roasting and frying.

PARSLEY

Parsley is an essential ingredient in the kitchen garden for its flavour
and versatility. It has a fresh flavour that goes particularly well with
fish, and chopped parsley is often used as a garnish. Parsley is
a feature in most potato salads, adding fresh taste and colour
(see the recipe for 'Lyonnaise salad' at the end of the chapter).
Although technically biennial, it's generally grown as an annual.
You should be able to grow and pick fresh parsley at most times of the
year. The curly-leaved varieties are particularly attractive and make
a wonderful edging or border to the flower or vegetable garden. Italian,
or flat-leaf, parsley has a stronger flavour than curled varieties.

GARLIC

Garlic (*Allium sativum*) is widely cultivated for culinary use and is recognisable by its
pungent smell and flavour. It tastes great roasted whole and is the perfect complement
to roast potato (see recipe for 'Roman potatoes' at the end of the chapter).
Garlic can be propagated in winter and early spring simply by planting the garlic cloves that we use
in the kitchen. Pick the biggest, healthiest looking bulbs and break them into cloves. Plant them
4–8 cm deep, 15 cm apart and pointy end up. Sunshine, good drainage and moisture are essential
for success, but ease off on watering towards the end of the season. When the foliage dries and withers
it's a sign that the bulbs are ready to be harvested (usually six to eight months after planting).
Harvest and wash mature bulbs, then leave them to dry in a cool airy place for a week or more.

My favourite varieties

Kipfler is an elongated potato with yellow skin, light yellow flesh and what I would describe as
a pleasant nutty flavour. It is best boiled or steamed and tossed into salads, but also makes a good
roasting potato.

Nicola has yellow skin and deep yellow flesh that has a distinctly 'buttery' flavour. Excellent boiled,
steamed or mashed, it is an absolute hit in our 'Nicola potato strudel with caraway' recipe.

King Edward is an oval- to pear-shaped potato with lovely cream and pink-blushed skin. The creamy
white flesh has a firm, waxy texture, making it ideal for boiling. It is also lovely baked or roasted, and
can be harvested mid to late season when the stems and leaves have withered.

Otway Red is an excellent all-purpose variety with red skin and pure white flesh. Serve it Roman style,
seasoned with salt, pepper, rosemary and garlic, and roasted until golden brown. It is delicious mashed.

Pink Eye does as much for the eye as the tastebuds, with purple skin and creamy yellow flesh. It makes
a delicious mash, and the 'new' potatoes are tasty boiled and tossed into salads.

Lyonnaise salad

Serves 4

6 Pink Eye potatoes, washed
1 medium brown onion, sliced
3 rashers bacon, diced
4 mustard leaves or $\frac{1}{2}$ bunch of curly endive
1 tablespoon parsley, chopped
1 tablespoon butter
Sea salt and ground pepper, to taste
125 ml vinaigrette (see page 189)

1. Parboil the potatoes for 15 minutes,
then drain and cut into 1 cm-thick slices.
2. Heat the butter in a heavy-based pan and sauté
the potatoes until golden. Remove potatoes from
heat and set aside in a bowl.
3. Sauté the onion and bacon until tender.
4. Place the sautéed onion and bacon in the bowl
with the potatoes, and dress with the vinaigrette
while still hot. Mix through the leaves and
parsley, and serve.

Roman potatoes

Serves 6

1 kg Otway Red or Nicola potatoes
¼ cup plain flour
1 whole garlic bulb
3 sprigs rosemary
1 cup sunflower oil
Sea salt and ground pepper, to taste

1. Dice the potatoes into 2-cm pieces, coat with
flour and season with salt and pepper.
2. Place the potatoes in a roasting tray and scatter
the rosemary sprigs and unpeeled garlic cloves.
3. Pour the oil over potatoes and garlic and toss
it through, then cook in a moderate oven for
approximately 40 minutes, or until golden.

Nicola potato strudel with caraway

Serves 6 as an entree, or more as an accompaniment to a main course.

1 kg Nicola potatoes

4 large red or brown onions

1 tablespoon olive oil

125 g butter

1 tablespoon brown sugar

1 tablespoon red wine vinegar

2 tablespoons caraway seeds

Salt and pepper, to taste

4 sheets butter puff pastry

60 g butter, melted

2 tablespoons breadcrumbs

1. Preheat the oven to 180°C. Slice the onions and slowly sauté with oil and butter on low heat until lightly caramelised. Add the brown sugar and the red wine vinegar. Remove from heat. Peel and dice the potatoes, then parboil until just cooked. Drain and roughly mash the potatoes. Stir in the caraway seeds and caramelised onion, and season with salt and pepper.

2. Lay out two pastry sheets, brush the edges with water and overlap with the remaining two sheets to form a seam, in effect making two long sheets. Place the potato mixture in a line down the long side of each pastry sheet, and carefully roll the sheets to form two long sausages. Place both on a baking tray with the seam side down. Brush with melted butter, score with a knife point and sprinkle breadcrumbs on top.

3. Bake for 25–35 minutes until the pastry is puffed and the butter bubbling. Allow to cool slightly before cutting.

Leafy greens

My uncle and aunt have a wonderful kitchen garden, overflowing with all sorts of vegetables, herbs and edible flowers. When I'm over there for dinner they hand me a colander and paring knife and send me into the garden to harvest the salad. Part of the fun is mixing varieties and flavours together, and then identifying each as the meal progresses.

By leafy greens I mean staple salad ingredients like lettuce, rocket, chicory and endives. There are also lots of Asian greens to try, offering a variety of tastes, textures and aromas. There is a multitude of varieties to choose from for your kitchen garden, but for a constant supply of leafy greens go for a combination of fast developers, like rocket, along with several varieties of lettuce.

Among the lettuces that make hearts are the cos varieties, with long, heavily ribbed leaves and a crunchy texture, and the more compact butterheads and crispheads, including the common Iceberg. From a purely practical point of view I prefer to grow the loose-leaf or cutting types of lettuce, such as Lollo Rosso and Royal Oak Leaf, because I can nip into the garden and pick a few leaves as I need them and the plant keeps on growing.

Another wonderful salad ingredient is rocket (*Eruca sativa*), an annual from the Mediterranean which has the appearance of watercress. The young leaves are tastiest and have a wonderful bitey flavour which really stands out in the salad mix.

Chicory (*Chicorium intybus*) brings colour and crunch to salads. It is native to Europe and is closely related to endive, lettuce and sunflowers. Until I grew them my sole experience of chicory was the crunchy white witlof variety you find at the markets (my dad still makes the most delicious orange and witlof salad). I've since discovered many other kinds, including a variety of red chicory, commonly known by its Italian name, radicchio, which starts off green and becomes red as the season progresses. The bitterness is more pronounced in the red leaves, and the inner leaves are milder than the outer ones. If you're after something a little less bitter, try one of the green chicories, known as sugar loaf chicories. These are non-heading types whose texture and appearance resembles cos lettuce, and they respond well to cut-and-come-again treatment. You can also find attractive variegated varieties of chicory, with streaked, speckled or striped leaves.

Health and nutrition

Leafy greens are an abundant source of vitamin C, potassium, iron, calcium and dietary fibre. They are also rich in beta-carotene and other antioxidants with infection- and cancer-fighting properties. More commonly associated with yellow and orange vegetables, the beta-carotene is masked by the green pigment chlorophyll. To get the highest levels, go for those with the darkest green leaves. Leafy greens are low in carbohydrates and fat, and contain vitamin K, which is essential for normal blood clotting.

Growing

Leafy greens give you a bumper crop in a short amount of time for little effort. Choose a sunny spot, keep the water up and provide well-drained soil rich in organic matter. Leafy crops are nitrogen-greedy and will enjoy a complete liquid feed every few weeks during the growing season. I enjoy the diverse range of colours and textures of leafy greens dotted around the garden and in pots on the balcony—an excellent way of growing them if you don't need huge quantities.

In regions that don't get heavy frosts, lettuces can be grown year-round in a well-drained soil with plenty of manure and compost worked in beforehand. Seed can be direct-sown and later thinned out, or germinated in pots and transplanted as young seedlings. In cold climates, seed can be sown in late winter or early spring in a greenhouse or under glass. Once the soil has warmed and frost has passed, you can make successive sowings outdoors until August. Of course, you can also buy the seedlings in punnets at your nursery or garden centre.

With some consideration of variety, it is possible to grow chicory throughout the year in most climates. In general, chicory is a biennial plant with a thick taproot and a mostly tight head of leaves. The whole head can be harvested by cutting a few centimetres above the taproot (so it can re-sprout), and the leaves have a pleasantly bitter flavour.

The closely related endive (*Cichorium endivia*) is usually grown as an annual and has a looser growing habit. In cooler regions endives may be grown through most of the year. In warmer areas I'd suggest growing it as an autumn or winter crop, because it has a tendency to bolt in hot conditions. They make excellent cut-and-come-again crops, and have a slightly spicy flavour.

Asian greens are among some of the easiest leafy greens to grow. Although they are becoming more widely available as seedlings, Asian herbs and vegetables grow very easily from seed. In cooler regions

Leafy greens give you a bumper crop in a short amount of time for little effort

the seed of many varieties can be sown in spring, when the danger of frost has passed. Like most leafy greens, they will quickly bolt to seed in hot, dry weather.

Harvest

Make it a ritual to nip into the garden just before lunch or dinner and harvest your leafy greens so they're utterly fresh. Many varieties are cut-and-come-again, which refers to a plant's ability to re-sprout from an undisturbed root. As long as the plant is not uprooted, it will re-grow after the first head or mature leaves are cut, allowing you to repeat-harvest over an extended growing period.

When it comes to thinning your crop, don't discard the young plants. Immature leafy greens are particularly tasty in salads and stir-fries.

Kitchen

Leafy greens are the basis for a variety of tasty salad combinations. Pick a balance of mild and strong flavours so one variety doesn't dominate the mix, and toss in a few edible flowers like nasturtiums or violas for colour.

Some varieties, particularly the Asian greens, can also be lightly steamed or stir-fried. The secret is to avoid overcooking, which destroys both their taste and appearance. For me, a simple way to enjoy them is to briefly sauté them in a very hot pan, season with sea salt and lemon juice, and garnish with toasted pumpkin, sunflower or sesame seeds.

My favourite varieties

Red Velvet is one of the prettiest loose-leaf varieties of lettuce available, with luxurious deep red foliage and a velvety texture. Being a loose-leaf variety, leaves can be harvested throughout the growing season as you need them. It also has the added advantage of being slow to bolt. To create impact, plant Red Velvet in bold groups in the vegetable or flower garden, and add it to salads for colour and variety.

Freckles is a distinctive and attractive variety of cos lettuce, with unusual speckled leaves, upright form and crunchy midribs. It's a great contrast to green-leafed lettuce, both in the garden and the kitchen, and makes unique Caesar salad.

Gold Rush is an incredibly decorative loose-leaf variety of lettuce with crinkly lime green leaves, and has a lovely mild flavour that brings unique texture to salads. Pick the leaves as you need them.

Radicchio Red Treviso comes from the Italian province Treviso, famed for its fertile agricultural land and local specialties such as White Chicory and Red-Claret Radicchio. It is a splendid looking vegetable whose leaves turn a rich burgundy colour in the cooler weather. Whole or torn, Red Treviso leaves are a striking addition to the salad bowl, but make sure you balance its bitterness with other leafy greens. The cup-like leaves are also perfect for holding salads or vegetables. It stores well and will keep for up to a month in the refrigerator.

Five-Colour Silverbeet is an easy grower with brilliantly coloured red, orange, yellow, pink or white stems, which can be harvested as needed for months. The leaves and stems can be used in colourful salads, stews and soups. Five-Colour makes a real impact in the garden, planted in groups to provide a mass of vibrant, jostling stems. You can also grow an attractive selection in pots and window boxes.

ASIAN GREENS

Pak Choi is wonderful to grow because it is vigorous and robust. Also known as Chinese White Cabbage or Bok Choy, Pak Choi is leafy, juicy and mild-tasting, with a delicate hot flavour. Both the stems and leaves of Pak Choi are used in Asian cuisine, and make delicious stir-fries, soups and salads. There are both pale green and white-stemmed varieties, with thick, crisp stalks. There is little difference in flavour between the two varieties, so the choice may simply come down to the look you'd like to achieve on the plate. Pak Choi is fast growing and ready to harvest in as little as 40 days from sowing.

Tat Soi (Chinese Flat Cabbage) was the first of the Asian greens that I grew. You'll recognise it as the round, glossy, dark green leaf that you get in the mesclun mix at the supermarket. As a plant it has white stems that lay almost flat on the ground. The stems and leaves of Tat Soi have a more intense flavour than Pak Choi, but can be used in much the same way in many Asian dishes.

Wong Bok (the hybrid Chinese Cabbage) has large barrel-shaped hearts and delicate green and white crinkled leaves. It has a sweeter flavour than traditional European cabbage and makes a wonderful addition to hearty soups, or stir-fried with other crisp Asian vegetables. Chinese cabbages are ready to harvest when the heads are firm and full but not too hard, which may take up to 100 days. You can also selectively remove outside leaves as the plant grows.

Mizuna and *Mibuna* are peppery Japanese greens that add distinctive flavour to salads, soups and stir-fries. The two are closely related, but Mizuna is distinguished by frizzled or serrated leaves and Mibuna by smooth edges. They perform in pots just as well as in the garden, and grow with furious energy.

Asian greens and black bean vinaigrette

Makes about 3 cups of vinaigrette

250 g mixed Asian greens, rinsed
salt and ground pepper, to taste

Black bean vinaigrette
50 g black beans
200 ml sherry vinegar
450 ml peanut oil
1 teaspoon sugar
30 ml port
A trace of sesame oil

1. Place the ingredients into a lidded jar and shake to combine. Glaze the mixed Asian greens with black bean vinaigrette and serve.

Five-Colour Silverbeet with orange blossom oil

Serves 4

8 large stems of Five-Colour Silverbeet
2 teaspoons orange blossom oil (see page 163)
Pinch of sea salt
Freshly ground pepper, to taste

1. Trim the leaf away from the stems and julienne the stems. Steam the leaves and stems for two minutes.
2. Place the stems and leaves in a bowl and mix orange blossom oil through. Season with sea salt and ground pepper.

Rocket with oven-roasted tomatoes

250 g rocket leaves
2 tablespoons olive oil
1 tablespoon balsamic vinegar
Salt and pepper, to taste

Note: See recipe for Oven-roasted
Tomatoes on page 31 for preparation
of tomatoes.

1. Dress rocket leaves with olive oil and balsamic
vinegar, and season with salt and pepper.
2. Place the rocket leaves next to the tomatoes
and serve.

Vinaigrette dressing

Makes about 3 cups

3 garlic cloves
3 anchovy fillets
100 ml balsamic vinegar
1 tablespoon Dijon mustard
1 teaspoon raw sugar
1 teaspoon finely grated orange zest
1 tablespoon finely chopped parsley
2 teaspoons tahini
freshly ground black pepper, to taste
1 teaspoon sea salt
600 ml olive oil

1. Place all the ingredients except for the oil
into a food processor and process until smooth.
2. With the motor running, slowly add the oil.
3. Taste and add a little more oil if you like.

Potted feast

Don't think that just because your space is small you can't grow and harvest your own fresh fruit and vegetables. There are plenty of delicious varieties that are tailor-made to grow in containers. There have been times in my life when all I had to work with was a small balcony. This obviously posed a few challenges and frustrations for an enthusiastic gardener like myself, but with a little creativity and effort I was able to enjoy a potted garden that supplied fresh produce throughout the year. There was never a shortage of fresh herbs, salad greens and Asian vegetables. I also had great results with baby beets, carrots, potatoes and cherry tomatoes, and was even able to harvest full-sized fruit from miniature trees. By chopping, changing and experimenting from season to season I was able to feel like I was really gardening!

I've talked about my balcony experience here, but I'm really trying to emphasise what can be achieved in any space when gardening in pots. Vegetables will grow in just about any container—polystyrene boxes, plastic pots, decorative planters, window boxes, you name it. I favour bigger containers. In a tiny courtyard or balcony larger pots will maximise your space more effectively than lots of smaller ones, which can tend to look cluttered and messy. Large containers are also better able to withstand the drying effects of sun and wind. You could create a stylish modern look by sticking to materials or colours that complement your home, or try a combination of containers in different colours or styles to create visual impact or contrast. There's no reason why you can't achieve good results with some vegetables in hanging baskets, too, but remember that they are up high and exposed, so they will get very thirsty.

The size and depth of the container will affect your choice of plant. As a rough guide, those with shallow roots, such as lettuce, require a depth of 20–25 centimetres, while bigger crops like tomatoes, and root crops such as carrot and beetroot, perform better with a soil depth of at least 30–40 centimetres. Small fruit trees may need more depth again.

Growing

There are a few fundamentals for achieving success when growing fruit and vegetables in containers. The starting point is to use good-quality potting mix. Pots have a tendency to dry out quickly, so it's wise to choose a mix that contains a wetting agent and water-storing crystals, or alternatively you can add these products separately.

Some crops are more dry-tolerant than others, but generally you will need to water your containers often, probably every day during hot, dry weather. I like the experience of hand-watering my pots, but drip systems can be installed to save time and water. With continual watering, nutrients are quickly leached from pots, so plants should be liquid-fed regularly. Leafy vegetables like lettuce and silverbeet particularly benefit from a good nitrogen-based liquid fertiliser every few weeks.

Another key to success is the availability of sunlight—at least five to six hours a day for most crops. One of the great advantages of containers is that they can be moved around to capture sunlight or provide shelter, depending on the particular needs of each variety.

Root crops are happy in pots, provided the container is deep enough. Mini varieties of root crops or naturally compact vegetables are obviously good choices for growing in pots. The dwarf or baby varieties are especially delightful and a favourite with kids. They're also often tastier because the flavour is concentrated.

Certainly some of the easiest vegetables to grow in pots are compact, fast-growing leafy crops like Asian greens, lettuce and silverbeet, which can be grown year-round in most regions. Cut-and-come-again vegetables like these are most satisfying, providing a continuous supply of salad greens.

My favourite varieties

Root crops and mini varieties

Beetroot can be grown confidently in pots. Mini Gourmet is a good option, producing tasty, golf ball-sized beets in about six weeks. The leafy tops can also be used in salads.

Radish performs well in pots, and is a good option for introducing kids to gardening because they can see results in a short space of time (you may even get them to eat one!). Try Easter Egg Radishes for their colourful pink, purple, red and white roots.

Carrots can be grown well in pots, with the short, thick types and baby varieties doing exceptionally well in containers about 30 centimetres deep. Baby is one of the best varieties, with small sweet carrots ready to be harvested in just 10–12 weeks. Another good option is the heirloom Mini Round Carrot.

There are plenty of delicious varieties that are tailor-made to grow in containers

Capsicum grows well in larger pots and tubs. It makes a handsome container plant in its own right and loves the heat. Try mini sweet capsicums with sweet tasty peppers.

Chillies are wonderfully decorative in pots, providing fiery red, green, yellow and purple fruits. Those with more adventurous tastebuds will love Jalapeno Fire Eater or the Bird's Eye varieties.

Mini tomatoes are ideally suited to smaller pots and can be used in hanging baskets, too. Silvery Fir Tree is a good compact variety for pots, with masses of tasty red salad tomatoes, or try Sweet Tumbler, which will cascade out of containers and hanging baskets.

Leafy crops

Lettuces are available in a wide range of decorative leaf shapes, colours and flavours. The outside leaves can be picked as you need them. Some to try are Red Velvet or Royal Oak Leaf, or Freckles, a compact cos variety with a striking spotted leaf pattern. You can mix several varieties together in a larger pot for a stunning effect.

Rocket is another fast-growing favourite, with spicy leaves that are perfect in salads.

Asian greens are often ideally suited to containers, and grow with furious energy. Mizuna and Mibuna are delicious Japanese greens with a spicy flavour that grow easily from seed. Pak Choi is another relaxed pot variety perfect for salads and stir-fries.

Silverbeet is wonderfully productive in pots. The heirloom Five-Colour is a favourite for its looks as well as its flavour, with delicious red, yellow, orange, pink, white or bicolour stems.

Tasty and colourful companions

There are also some wonderful opportunities for introducing herbs and flowers to your potted vegetable garden, which bring colour and texture to the planting.

Edible flowers such as nasturtiums are perfect companions. As a kid I had nasturtium leaves in my sandwiches every day for lunch—Vegemite, cheese and nasturtium leaves. You might not rush off to try that combination yourself, but the leaves and flowers are also great in salads. Calendulas are another highly decorative option and create a beautiful tapestry among vegetables and herbs in the potted kitchen garden. The golden flower heads look spectacular in salads, too.

Herbs such as oregano, basil, chives, mint, thyme, rosemary and parsley introduce colour, texture and flavour, and all of them are pleasantly fragrant. In the right spot most herbs will grow in containers as successfully as they do in the garden. Mint is certainly one herb that is actually best confined to a container to control its overenthusiastic growing habits.

Herbs are a natural companion to vegetables, both in the garden and the kitchen. Pots of tomatoes, basil, oregano and parsley will give a Mediterranean air to terraces and balconies, or you can fill Eastern-inspired containers with coriander, chillies and Asian greens.

SPACE SAVERS

Cool-season vegetables with big heads like broccoli and cauliflower
can take up a lot of space in containers and take longer to mature,
but before you discount them altogether it's worth investigating
mini varieties with more compact heads.
Other vegetables with space-saving qualities include non-running forms of
pumpkin, melon and cucumber, which won't take over and outgrow the space.
Try pumpkin varieties such as Golden Nugget, with deep yellow flesh, or mini
Delicata (heirloom), with a compact vine and small, sweet potato-tasting fruit.
You might also like to grow the green-fleshed mini rockmelon Ha-ogen.
Growing taller crops or climbing varieties can be a bit more complicated,
but you can succeed if you provide strong support and use large containers.

ROSEMARY

You could plant rosemary for its ornamental value alone. It's an evergreen
shrub with aromatic grey-green foliage and deep blue, pale blue or white
flowers, depending on the variety. Rosemary brings a Mediterranean feel
to the garden. It makes an elegant shrub in pots and containers and can
be clipped for a formal look. Use it to create hedges around the formal
herb garden or flower border. There are also ground-hugging prostrate
species which spread to form a carpet of colour and fragrance.
In the kitchen, rosemary is the perfect complement to lamb, chicken and roasted
potatoes and pumpkin (see recipe for Roman Potatoes on page 175).

CHOICE
PEACHES

Preserving

At certain times of the year home gardeners may experience an abundance of fresh produce—particularly from bountiful summer and autumn crops. Faced with more than you can consume or give away, preserving is a great way to make the most of a surplus harvest and enjoy your favourite fruit and vegetables out of season.

Bottling

Fruit preserving may be an old tradition, but many people are rediscovering bottling as a method of preserving fruit and vegetables, and it's easy to see why. For starters, just take a look at the label on many commercial foods. It's likely you'll find a long list of preservatives and other additives. Bottling your own fruit means you can control what you put in—and there's no need for chemicals, preservatives, or even sugar.

If you're daunted by the idea of preserving, don't be. It is not a complex process and today's equipment makes bottling quicker and simpler than it's ever been. For a modest investment of time and expense, you end up with delicious preserved fruit that can be enjoyed throughout the year, particularly out of season. Rows of bottled produce are also incredibly decorative.

Bottling relies on forming an effective vacuum seal. Through the heating and expansion process, surplus air is expelled and, as the bottles cool, a vacuum is formed. The contents of the bottle are sterilised and are effectively preserved.

Preserving vegetables can be complex so, for the novice, fruit bottling is the best place to start. Traditionally, fruit was preserved in thick sugary syrup, but I tend to avoid using this because there are plenty of natural sugars in the fruit, and there are other healthier alternatives. Most fruit is full of natural acids, and it's the acid that helps ensure safe preservation. Some fruits, like pears, tomatoes and figs, have lower acid levels, so lemon juice or citric acid needs to be added to help them keep.

Fruit is best selected ripe and should always be washed first. Peel and slice the fruit or use it whole—it's up to you. Damaged fruit can also be preserved, either as puree or by cutting the bad bits out.

Suitable varieties

Clingstone peach varieties, such as Golden Queen, have a firm texture that makes them ideal for bottling. Other good preserving fruits that can be grown successfully in the home garden include

apricots, cherries, pears and plums—particularly the European plum varieties, like President or Greengage, prune types such as Prune d'Agen, or the Japanese blood plum Satsuma.

TOOLS OF THE TRADE

You'll need these essential items, available at hardware shops and homeware outlets.

Bottling jars: Use only bottles and lids made specifically for preserving. Always wash the bottles thoroughly before filling. They can be used over and over again, but don't use them if they are cracked or damaged.

Lids: Stainless steel lids are best because they don't rust. Always wash them well before you use them.

Rubber rings: These rings help to seal the jars and are best used new. Store them away from heat and light to prevent deterioration in the rubber.

Clips: You'll need a single spring clip to seal each bottle. Clips last for a number of years.

Preserving kits: Today's electric kits make preserving really easy.

HOW TO BOTTLE FRUIT

There are traditional methods of stove-top bottling that don't require too much specialist equipment, but you need to monitor temperatures and time carefully to ensure that any harmful micro-organisms are destroyed. For me, a small outlay for a commercial preserving kit is well worth it. It makes bottling a simple and quick process that achieves reliable results.

For safe and effective preserving, follow the directions that come with your preserving kit. While the process may vary slightly from kit to kit, the major steps are outlined below.

1. Clean your preserving jars and check for imperfections that may stop proper sealing. Soak the rubber rings in water for 15 minutes, then carefully stretch them over the mouth of the jar.

2. Place the fruit in the jars, along with the water, fruit juice, liqueur or sugar syrup. Try to pack the fruit fairly tightly, with the cut surface to the centre of the bottle and the fruit in a spiral pattern, so you get a nice effect from the outside. The trick with the liquid is to add it as you go so air pockets don't form.

3. Leave a little bit of space at the top of the bottle—say 1 cm or so—then put the lid on. Make sure you can't see the rubber ring; this way you know the lid is on properly. Apply your clip across the centre of the lid, making sure it is firmly in place.

4. Place the bottles into the preserving kit, then fill it with water so the bottles are entirely covered and plug it in. Different sized bottles will vary in their processing time, so read the kit directions carefully. The water should not be allowed to boil.

5. At the end of the process, release the hot water via the side tap. Carefully remove the jars from the kit while they're still hot, making sure you don't lift them by the lid. Leave the bottles to cool for 12–18 hours on a wooden cutting board, then carefully remove the clips and gently pull the seal to ensure it is still firm. Preserved fruit is at its best for about a year.

PRESERVING VEGETABLES

If you're blessed with a bumper crop, don't waste it. While vegetables are a little harder to preserve, given they are not as acidic as fruit and naturally don't last as long, your efforts will be rewarded. By using herbs, spices, quality vinegar and olive oil, the flavours will infuse into the vegetables. Mushrooms, capsicum, asparagus, artichokes and courgettes all preserve well.

Always use unblemished produce and process it as soon as you can. A common way to preserve vegetables is to clean them with a pinch of bicarbonate of soda in water and dry. Then grill, dry or boil the vegetables in vinegar (red or white wine varieties work well). Place the cooled vegetables in sterile jars with lemon juice and herbs or spices to taste, and fill the jar with olive oil. Make sure the oil covers the vegetables. Air bubbles can support the growth of bacteria, so eliminate them by gently stirring the vegetables after they are immersed in the oil—just don't stir too vigorously because it may have the opposite effect. Once satisfied, seal your jars and store. Leave them for two to six weeks before consuming to allow the flavours to develop. Once the jar is opened keep refrigerated and use the contents quickly, within a week or so.

JAMS, PICKLES AND CHUTNEYS

There's nothing more satisfying than making your own chutneys, pickles, jams and jellies, and stocking your pantry with delectable preserves. Preserves provide an extended reward for your gardening labours. They are easy to make, delicious to eat and make the most of your surplus seasonal crops. Use green or vine-ripened tomatoes in traditional chutneys, tangy limes in hot pickles, or make luscious fruit jams.

Strawberry jam

Makes 3 jars

500 g ripe heirloom strawberries
700 g caster sugar
¼ teaspoon tartaric acid

1. Rinse, drain and hull the strawberries.
2. Place in pan and, without adding any liquid, cook gently over a low heat for approximately 12 minutes.
3. Add sugar and tartaric acid to strawberry mixture and stir until dissolved. Boil rapidly until setting stage is reached, approximately 10 minutes.
4. While still warm, fill sterilised jars with jam.
5. Seal immediately.

Tomato relish

Makes 10 jars

3 kg ripe tomatoes, such as Amish Paste, chopped

1 kg brown onions, sliced

2 tablespoons curry powder

1 kg raw sugar

1 tablespoon salt

$^{1}/_{2}$ teaspoon cayenne pepper

1 tablespoon mustard powder

500 ml brown vinegar

1. Place all ingredients into a stainless steel preserving pan and bring to simmering point.
2. Simmer for approximately 1 $^{1}/_{2}$ hours, stirring occasionally to stop mixture from burning.
3. Remove from heat and lightly puree the relish to thicken, but ensure that some texture remains in the relish sauce.
4. Place into sterilised jars and seal immediately. Store for one month before using to allow flavours to develop.

Freezing

Freezing is another option for extending the life of surplus produce for up to six months. Some fruits and vegetables, like apples, tomatoes and plums, can be cooked, pureed and cooled, then frozen in tubs for later use in soups, sauces or desserts. Others, such as beans, peppers and broccoli, can be blanched for a few minutes in salted boiling water, then cooled and frozen in plastic bags. Some produce with high-water content like lettuce and cucumbers don't take well to freezing because the swollen ice crystals damage their flesh.

Many berries also have a good reputation for freezing. Blueberries can be frozen in containers or bags without clumping together, so you can remove individual berries as you need them. Others, like raspberries, will clump, so it's a good idea to freeze single layers on trays first, before transferring into freezer bags. Berries are great straight from the freezer—just like a healthy miniature sorbet!

Consuming thawed produce raw will rarely match its fresh equivalent, so as a general rule only freeze produce that you intend to cook with or use for jams, pickles or chutneys.

You can also freeze fresh herbs for a year-round supply. Strip the leaves from coarse herbs, like thyme, sage and rosemary, and pack them into freezer bags with as much air extracted as possible. Chop soft herbs, like basil, parsley and mint, and freeze in ice-cube trays topped with water, to use as you need them.

Nothing says 'celebration' like a delicious feast enjoyed with family and friends

Harvest
celebration

A feast from the garden

I can't think of a better way to celebrate any occasion than with a garden feast for family and friends. Transform the outdoors into your dining room. Accessorise the table with brightly coloured flowers and foliage, and serve up delicacies that you've cooked with produce picked fresh from the garden. Complete the scene with a simple table cloth, cushions and stylish glassware. As a final touch, decorate the garden with coloured lanterns. Hang them from a nearby tree or on stakes to give the garden a festive feel.

Menu one

STARTER
Roasted Baby Heirloom Beetroot with Persian Fetta (page 99)

MAIN
Pan Fried Salmon with Peach Relish (page 61)
Heronswood Tomato Salad (page 32)
Beans with Toasted Almonds and Burnt Butter (page 43)

DESSERT
Honey-Roasted Figs with Marscarpone, Pistachios and Orange (page 118)

Menu two

STARTER
Capsicum Stack (page 81)

MAIN
Breast of Organic Chicken with Bull's Blood Chard (page 98)
Roman Potatoes (page 175)
Broccolini with Anchovy Vinaigrette (page 146)

DESSERT
Mini Meringues with Lemon Curd (page 160)

About Heronswood

Heronswood is the home of the Digger's Club, which was founded by Clive and Penny Blazey in 1978 with the idea of supplying unusual plants and seeds to passionate gardeners. Digger's is now Australia's largest garden club and is committed to sustainable gardening.

Heronswood is located at Dromana on the Mornington Peninsula in Victoria, Australia, and the first gardens were planted here in the 1870s. The garden has extensive plantings of fruits and flowers, and there are now five separate vegetable gardens. It is from these gardens that we have rescued the best heirloom vegetable varieties described in *Garden Feast*.

Many would describe Heronswood as a cottage garden as if this refers only to the style of our flower planting, but it should also describe the inter-planting of vegetables, fruit, roses and herbs. It is this inter-planting that prevents the build up of pest problems. We are in the process of organically certifying our gardens.

The Mornington Peninsula is surrounded by water, which gives the area its maritime climate. In winter, the water in Port Phillip Bay retains heat which prevents frost, thus providing a longer growing season than found elsewhere in Victoria. We are also able to grow a wider range of sub-tropicals than you expect to see in Victoria.

If you come to visit Heronswood, don't be intimidated by the standard of gardening—our gardens are managed with a staff of three! Considering the area is equivalent to 25 house blocks, this equates to only five hours work each week for the typical gardener. To live in a beautiful garden and be self-sufficient is a wonderful reward for so little effort. Our gardens are also water efficient—we have cut our water use by 60 per cent in the last three years.

Much of the delicious food we grow in the garden is served in our Heronswood café, so not only can you see all the wonderful and rare foods growing, but you can taste them too. As much as possible we pick from the gardens for the café and we take the inspiration for the menu from what is ready in the garden. We serve food that is seasonal, and try to cook with ingredients that are regional and organic. We hope that you find the dishes in *Garden Feast* as pleasurable to grow and eat as we do!

Heronswood, 105 LaTrobe Parade, Dromana, Victoria, Australia, www.diggers.com.au

Index

Acknowledgements

I have always believed in surrounding myself with great people, and this book certainly would not have been possible if it hadn't been for my editor Nick Arnott, who was so generous with his friendship and talent and time. It was a dream of ours Nicky and we did it!

Special thanks to Clive and Penny Blazey and all the staff at Heronswood for their endless support and dedication to the project. I particularly thank Talei Kenyon, Jane Varkulevicius and Camilla Lazzar for sharing their incredible knowledge and for their generous assistance. To the staff at Heronswood Café, particularly Glenn Keogh, Antonia Love and Luke Palmer, thank you for creating the delicious recipes that showcase the flavours of the wonderful fruit and veg featured in this book—you all worked so tirelessly.

To Alan King and Jacky Forsyth for all the work you put into testing the recipes — it's a hard job guys, but someone's got to do it! To my family and friends who were dragged to numerous photo shoots — I hope the gorgeous food made up for it!

I'm so grateful that I was able to work with such an incredibly talented photographer, and someone who put their heart and soul into this project. Virginia, you were an absolute joy to work with and every single photo in this book is simply outstanding. Thank you so much.

Special thanks to my publishers, ABC Books, in particular Brigitta Doyle, for your guidance and wisdom. To Ellie Exarchos, thank you for your beautiful design. The book looks exactly the way I had always imagined and hoped it would. I also wish to thank my managers, Amanda and Sarah, for holding the fort while I spent days holed up writing. Where would I be without you!

Finally, to Alexandre Araujo for your love and support and for believing in me. Here's to many celebrations and feasts from the garden!

First published in the UK in 2008 by
APPLE PRESS
7 Greenland Street, London, NW1 0ND, United Kingdom
www.apple-press.com

ISBN 978 1 84543 253 9

First published in Australia by ABC Books for the
AUSTRALIAN BROADCASTING CORPORATION

A number of the photographs and aspects of the text appearing in
Garden Feast have been previously published in *Gardening Australia*
magazine. The author and publisher thank them for their kind
permission to reproduce the material in this book.

Edited by Nick Arnott
Additional editing by Catherine Taylor, Ali Levau, Susin Chow
and Tracy Rutherford
Photography by Virginia Cummins
Design and typesetting by Ellie Exarchos, Scooter Design
Colour reproduction by PageSet, Victoria, Australia
Printed in China by Imago

2 4 5 3 1